OPEN DOOR PREGNANCY CENTER
907 BAY RIDGE AVE.
TOMS RIVER, N. J. 08753
201-240-5504

THE OPEN DOOR PREGNANCY CENTER
50 HYERS ST.
TOMS RIVER, N.J. 08753
(908) 240-5504

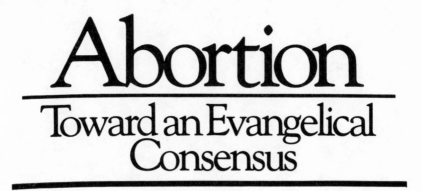

Abortion
Toward an Evangelical Consensus

PAUL B. FOWLER

MULTNOMAH · PRESS

Portland, Oregon 97266

Unless otherwise indicated, Scripture quotations are from the New American Standard Bible, © 1960, 1962, 1963, 1968, 1971, 1972, 1973, 1975, 1977 by the Lockman Foundation.

Scripture references marked NIV are from the Holy Bible: New International Version, © 1973, 1978, 1984 by the International Bible Society and published by Zondervan Bible Publishers.

Edited by Rodney L. Morris
Cover design and illustration by Britt Taylor Collins

ABORTION
© 1987 by Multnomah Press
Portland, Oregon 97266

Multnomah Press is a ministry of Multnomah School of the Bible, 8435 NE Glisan Street, Portland, Oregon 97266.

Printed in the United States of America

Library of Congress Cataloging-in-Publication Data

Fowler, Paul.
  Abortion: toward an evangelical concensus.

  Includes indexes.
  1. Abortion—Religious aspects—Christianity.
2. Evangelicalism—United States. 3. Abortion—United
States. I. Title.
HQ767.35.F69   1987   241'.6976   86-23717
ISBN 0-88070-173-0

87 88 89 90 91 92 – 10 9 8 7 6 5 4 3 2 1

To

CAMMA

Loving Wife

Ideal Mother

Contents

Foreword

Abortion: Toward an Evangelical Consensus portrays a genuine biblical perspective on the right-to-life issue, but it also comes from one who has a great compassion for life.

I had the privilege of working with Paul Fowler in Jackson, Mississippi, while I was at the Voice of Calvary ministries and he a professor at the Reformed Theological Seminary. Paul almost singlehandedly brought together white and black pastors to initiate a creative work toward the improvement of the quality of life for the poor in Jackson and throughout Mississippi. He served tirelessly on our board of directors and in other ways.

This book portrays the heart of one who not only talks about abortion as a political and popular issue, but who also lives his overall life in a prolife context—not just pro-white life, but prolife as God himself sees it.

This book is a celebration of life and a testimony to Paul's commitment.

Abortion: Toward an Evangelical Consensus could serve as a theological base for all who are asking, "Is prolife biblical?" Regardless of one's biblical or personal perspective on this issue, he should read this book before forming a final opinion.

Dr. John M. Perkins
President and Founder
The John M. Perkins Foundation for
    Reconciliation and Development
Pasadena, California

Preface

The situation is startling, to say the very least: one in four pregnancies today ends in abortion. Approximately two million abortions are performed annually in the United States; worldwide, the figure soars to fifty to seventy-five million.

Some say abortion is murder. Some say not. The debate between them is perhaps the most crucial ethical issue of our day. Unfortunately, it has spawned much more emotion than clear thinking. It has managed to create a civil war in the church of Jesus Christ where one might have expected a united front.

Could a united front be found in the church? Certainly it will not be found if our discussion fails to rise above the level of mere accusation. Indeed, even a re-examination of the fundamental arguments is not likely to be of much help to us now, though to some degree this is always necessary. The debate is now an old one and the basic lines of disagreement are clear (and rigidly fixed). Somehow we must find a way to move beyond this impasse. I believe such a way is found in examining the underlying concepts and assumptions of the basic prochoice arguments and in comparing them with Scripture.

Our debate must be characterized by love. But confrontation is also necessary. On an issue such as abortion, we must be clear as to where the problem lies. Moreover, the length of debate is morally relevant. When debate becomes an excuse for inaction, debate becomes immoral no matter how lofty the rhetoric. So we are pressing for a consensus and also for concerted action on behalf of both victims—the unborn child and the mother in distress.

11

I know this book will not end the debate. That is unrealistic. But it is my fervent prayer that these pages, in addressing the questions raised by abortion, will help promote both clear thinking on the issue and unity in Christ's church. I have attempted to clarify the scriptural, logical, and biological assumptions made by both the prolife and prochoice factions. In so doing, I have come to a strong position on the topic. I hope, when you have finished this slim volume, you will share my understanding.

*   *   *   *   *

Before proceeding, I wish to thank some extraordinary people. I am most of all thankful to my wife, Camma, and my two sons, Paul and John, for their patience and encouragement while I was writing this book. I am also very thankful to my niece, Mrs. Sue Zitzman, whose professional editing and guidance made this manuscript readable. I am also indebted to several special friends who read the manuscript: to Dr. Mark Ross, whose keen and logical insights were so helpful; to Rev. Curt Young, executive director of the Christian Action Council, whose knowledge of the issues kept me from making too many mistakes; and to Rev. Norman Bendroth, former director of communications of the Christian Action Council, whose insightful comments helped guide me. I also appreciate the encouragement and advice of Mr. Wave Nunnally, who read the manuscript in its early stages.

Finally, I wish to thank Multnomah Press, and especially my editor, Rod Morris, for the encouragement and support he has given me in the process of publishing this book.

Chapter 1

Why Can't We Agree?

> The strife is o'er, the battle done;
> The church has split, and our side won.

*T*his parody of a well-known old hymn[1] makes us laugh—albeit a bit nervously. Most humor hides a more serious concern beneath its surface, and this joke has its darker side too.

A church split is an ugly thing. I know. I've observed several of them. Each side claims superior spiritual knowledge and hurls harsh accusations at the other. After the mudslinging, many of the believers involved are left cynical and disillusioned; some leave the faith altogether. Most Christians would agree that consensus, whenever possible, is preferable to dissension, both for the health of a church and for its witness to the world. And this is even more true of the universal church than of an individual congregation.

One issue causing major rifts in the church today is abortion. On this subject we desire consensus, not only for the church and its witness but also for the sake of the unborn, whose lives hang in the balance. Every time another unborn child is aborted in America, the present wide-open policy of abortion-on-demand becomes more intolerable.

"Wait a minute," you may say. "You just mentioned abortion-on-demand. I'm against that, and so are most Christians. Isn't that a consensus?"

Since the 1970s, a number of positive signs suggest that a consensus *is* developing. Virtually everyone in the evangelical wing of the church is against abortion-on-demand. The prolife movement has drawn together such diverse groups as the Moral Majority and Evangelicals for Social Action, and found a voice in magazines such as *Moody Monthly* as well as *Sojourners*.

Yet we have also witnessed some sharp disagreements among evangelicals over abortion. Some prolife leaders, in their zeal to defend the unborn, rail against other Christians who have failed to adopt a clear-cut stand against all abortions. Those attacked then fight back with charges of their own.

Many Christian colleges and Bible schools hold no official position on the abortion issue. Yet often the faculty of these schools must sign a pledge every year vowing not to smoke or drink—minor issues in comparison.

Christianity Today, a major voice for evangelicalism, has allowed quotes such as the following to appear in its editorials:

> An absolutist prohibition of abortion will never secure political acceptance in our pluralistic society, and even many of us evangelicals would deem it undesirable. Evangelicals ought to agree to support any governmental action that would protect unborn children by making free abortions illegal. It may well be possible to outlaw abortions for trifling causes and all abortions beyond the first trimester except to save the life of the mother. The art of compromise is not sinful, it is usually realistic and often thoroughly Christian.[2]

Some Christian leaders continue to make statements such as, "I am personally opposed to abortion, but . . ." On the surface this sounds not like a prolife stance but prochoice rhetoric.

On the other side of the rift, prolife activist Franky

Schaeffer V accuses such persons and groups of ambivalence or even hostility to the prolife cause:

> More than ten years have passed since *Roe* v. *Wade*, yet consciousness of the evil of abortion is just beginning to be raised in many evangelical circles. This awareness has largely come from the influence of sources outside of the mainstream of the evangelical establishment, not from its leaders. Most of those evangelicals speaking out now about abortion are regrettably tardy, and there are still vast numbers of evangelicals remaining silent altogether on the issue of abortion. Worse yet, a substantial coterie of evangelical leaders are openly expounding theological, sociological and political excuses for why they have not adopted a clear pro-life position, seeking to make their wavering and compromising stance palatable for their evangelical followers.[3]

Those on the receiving end of Schaeffer's type of criticism respond that he and his cohorts are absolutists, extremists, hysterical, uncompromising.

Clearly we have not yet arrived at a consensus.

How long should it take for us to decide right and wrong on an issue of this magnitude? There is a growing frustration among many evangelicals about this lack of concerted action regarding abortion. Time has now become a moral consideration. A lack of resolve grows more and more inexcusable when the consequences (approximately two million abortions each year) are so grave.

We have not yet arrived at a consensus on abortion. Yet I see hope for unity in time. As more information is presented and discussed, I see an evangelical consensus growing. My hope is that open-minded reading and discussion of this book will further heal this rift between believers.

To begin the healing, we need to diagnose the problem. Where did the rift come from, this prolife versus prochoice split that seems to run through all levels of the church and of society as well? When you read the church's historical stance on this issue, you may be surprised.

The ancients, it would appear, were opposed to abortion.[4] But by the golden age of Greece, mankind had "come of age." Religion was at a low ebb, and the superstitions of mythology were being shed for the more enlightened ideas of philosophy. Man was set on a pedestal, and individual freedom was cultivated. Some, in fact, call that age "the first enlightenment."

At that time, the great philosophers of the age, Plato and Aristotle, were in favor of allowing abortion. Plato believed that both abortion and infanticide should be practiced when "necessary." And abortion should be demanded, he said, when a woman is over forty years of age.[5]

Aristotle argued that families should limit the number of their children in order to combat overpopulation and poverty. Deformed infants should be left to die of exposure. For both philosophers, the interests of the state took precedence over the rights of the unborn.

Aristotle also theorized that life in the fetus began when all the distinct organs were "formed"—around forty days for males and ninety days for females, he said![6] Prior to these deadlines, abortion would be lawful, and unlawful thereafter. This distinction between an unformed and formed fetus has profoundly influenced a number of philosophers and theologians down through the centuries.

Abortion-inducing drugs and doctors who performed abortions were not unknown in Greek society. Many of the same motives we hear today for aborting a child were used then—the child was unwanted or illegitimate, the child threatened the health of the mother or threatened the family's economy.

This Hellenistic spirit of individual freedom conquered Rome. In the early Republic, the husband had absolute power over his family. He could often sell, mutilate, or even kill family members at will. He was allowed to abandon any female newborn or any handicapped infant of either sex.[7]

By Augustus's day, women possessed increased freedom. Their husbands no longer held such power over them. But this new liberty was accompanied by adultery, an increased divorce rate, and more abortions. Women obtained abortions either through taking drugs or pessaries, or through undergoing surgical procedures often fatal to the mother as well as the child.

CHRISTIAN CONSENSUS

Such was the ethical climate among the Gentiles when the apostle Paul preached in Athens or Rome or in any area deeply affected by Hellenism, such as Galatia. It may be, therefore, that when Paul wrote his negative list of deeds of the flesh in Galatians 5:19-21 ("immorality, impurity, sensuality, idolatry, sorcery [Greek: *pharmakeia*, which can mean 'drugs']") he was including an implicit reference to abortion. After all, *pharmakeia* was used in an ancient gynecology text to refer to an abortifacient.[8]

Whether Paul intended to imply abortion in this text is difficult to decide.[9] In any event, historically, *the early church stood united against abortion*. A host of early church fathers who opposed abortion can be cited—Tertullian, Origen, Cyprian, Ambrose, Jerome, Chrysostom, Augustine.[10] Hellenism was not able to conquer the early church on this issue.

A first-century catechism placed those who are "killers of the child, who abort the mold of God," between murderers and adulterers, all embarked on "the Way of Darkness."[11] Caesarius of Arles wrote, "No woman should take any drug to procure an abortion, because she will be placed before the judgment seat of Christ, whether she has killed an already born child or a conceived one."[12] Clement of Alexandria in the second century taught: "For those women who conceal sexual wantonness by taking stimulating drugs to bring on an abortion wholly lose their humanity along with the fetus."[13]

When Athenagoras, a Greek apologist for Christianity,

was called upon to address the emperor Marcus Aurelius in A.D. 177, he sought to answer the charge of cannibalism which stemmed from the Romans' misunderstanding of the Eucharist. He stated that Christians could not even look at a murder, much less participate in one. To prove his point, he continued:

> What reason would we have to commit murder when we say that women who induce abortions are murderers, and will have to give account of it to God?[14]

Nor did Christians stand alone in their opposition to abortion. The Jews were against it. And Hippocrates, a physician in ancient Greece who did not agree with his contemporary Plato, wrote an oath in which he promised in part: "I will give no deadly medicine to anyone if asked . . . and in like manner I will not give to a woman a pessary to produce an abortion."[15] Hippocrates was trying to reform the medical practices of his day. Some schools of Greek thought, notably the Stoics, supported the Christian ethic on this issue.

We find then a consensus in the early church against abortion. And after the "Christianization" of the Roman Empire by Constantine, church laws against abortion were passed. It is true that some of the church fathers accepted Aristotle's distinction between "formed" and "unformed" fetus, but they did not use this distinction to justify the killing of the unborn. Their position was against abortion. For example, Augustine held to this twofold view, but he wrote: "A fetus is conceived and is born by a divine work, not a human one."[16] Aquinas believed that whether a fetus was "formed" or not, abortion was a serious sin.[17]

The Reformation produced no break in this moral opposition to abortion. Subsequently, down through the centuries of Western civilization even to the 1950s, abortion was frowned upon at large within the Christian community. The great continental theologians of the twentieth century who dealt specifically with abortion—Karl Barth, Emil Brunner, Dietrich Bonhoeffer, Helmut Thielicke, and many more—opposed it.[18]

Abortion has been rare through most of American history. In fact, laws in most states have had provisions that fined or imprisoned any doctor who intentionally destroyed the life of an unborn child. Also, an unborn child was defined as a human being from the time of conception.[19]

But law and public opinion have changed, and the hallmark of this change was a now famous court case. In 1970, a woman using the pseudonym of Janet Roe filed suit to overturn a Texas law prohibiting abortion. The Texas Criminal Appeals Court ruled that the state of Texas "has a compelling interest to protect fetal life." But then the United States Supreme Court, on 22 January 1973, held seven to two that the Texas law was unconstitutional and that Janet Roe had a right to an abortion. Their reason: an unborn child is not a person with the right of equal protection under law, only a "potential person."

In defending its decision, the majority of the Supreme Court ignored much of the history we just reviewed. They deliberately chose to bypass and reject the Judeo-Christian tradition against abortion and instead based their proabortion stance on ancient Greek and Roman law favorable to abortion.[20] What a strange choice. Not only is our country indebted to the Judeo-Christian tradition of respect for life, but as Harold O. J. Brown has pointed out:

> If it were true that pre-Christian non-Jewish antiquity did altogether accept abortion in principle and in practice, that would not be a strong argument in favor of our doing likewise; the ancient world accepted quite a number of things that we rightly reject, e.g., the absolute right of the father to decide upon the death of his children, the practice of slavery, torture, and mutilation and the custom of gladiatorial combat.[21]

We could mention other ancient practices no one wants revived: innumerable crucifixions, burning human torches, the abandonment of newborns, and preferential treatment to male babies. Justice Blackmun and his colleagues chose a precedent of bloodshed and depreciation of life over and against the way of love and life.

Why then did they do it? Or better, since the justices were but children of their time, how could society in a relatively brief span of time (primarily the 1960s) make such a drastic turnabout in opinion that the majority of Americans polled by 1973 indicated they favored abortion, at least in certain cases? How could such a revolution in public opinion take place?

This is a hard question, and no response will be complete. Abortion did not merely arrive on the scene in 1973 due to the Supreme Court decision. The sixties were years of turmoil, and the abortion issue was part of that turmoil.[22] Prior to the sixties, most Americans, including evangelicals, were solidly against abortion. Although there was no huge grass roots movement, a number of influences combined to bring about the great change of public opinion we have witnessed.

VOICES FOR CHOICE

In 1962, the American Law Institute (ALI) completed a ten-year study that proposed, among other things, a reformation of abortion laws. Actually, its proposals were rather conservative from today's point of view. They recommended allowances for abortion only when the mother's life or health was threatened, when the fetus was deformed or mentally retarded, or in cases of rape or incest. All other abortions, they claimed, should be criminal offenses; moreover, no abortions would be justifiable after viability.[23]

Many today would consider themselves against abortion in general, yet hold that the exceptions cited by the American Law Institute are legitimate. It is instructive, therefore, to realize that these particular "hard cases" became the central force in the drive to legalize abortion.

In June 1967, the American Medical Association reversed its stance of some 108 years when its House of Delegates endorsed the ALI proposal. Formerly, they had condemned all abortions except those intended to save the life of the mother.[24]

Then in May 1968, the American College of Obstetricians and Gynecologists followed suit, approving similar policies. However, their statement read: "In determining whether or not there is such a risk to [a woman's] health, account may be taken of the patient's total environment, actual or reasonably foreseeable." This broadened the definition of "health" and allowed for taking account of such stress on a mother as is generated by overcrowding and inadequate housing, too many children, or other emotional and physical problems.[25]

The push for abortion was on! Planned Parenthood reversed its statement of 1964 that "abortion kills the life of a baby, once it has begun." By 1968, Planned Parenthood was arguing that abortion was necessary to prevent unwanted pregnancies.[26]

The National Organization of Women (NOW) was formed in 1966. Under the influence of Betty Friedan, the movement to liberate women was equated with "total reproductive freedom." Women, according to NOW, will never be equal to men unless they are free from childbearing responsibilities.

The American Civil Liberties Union (ACLU) added their voice to the proabortion forces in 1968 in the name of *individual freedom* for women. (The civil rights of the unborn were apparently overlooked.) Then in 1969, the National Association for Repeal of Abortion Laws (NARAL) was formed, and its members laid the groundwork for abortion-on-demand.

During this same span of time, society experienced an outpouring of articles and books favorable to abortion. Consultations were held such as the International Conference on Abortion in Washington, D.C., in September 1967. While participants affirmed broad statements respecting human life, views ranged from a complete crackdown on illegal abortions to abortion-on-demand to stopping the "copulation explosion."

As the debate continued, most polls showed public opinion inching more and more toward favoring abortion. A Gallup poll in 1967 showed that 21 percent of Americans approved abortion upon maternal preference. By 1969, that figure had risen to 40 percent. The idea that abortion should be a private matter solely between a woman and her doctor was gaining acceptance.

Another survey conducted by the National Opinion Research Center in 1967 reported that 71 percent favored legal abortion when the mother's health was in danger, 56 percent when pregnancy was the result of rape or incest, and 55 percent when there was a strong possibility that the child would be born defective.

In 1970, Andie Knutson of the University of California revealed research which indicated that of a group of 350 health professionals surveyed, approximately 50 percent said a new life was already a human life by the end of the first trimester, 30 percent said it was not human until the second or third trimester, and 20 percent not until viable birth or later. Knutson noted that "religion and sex" were significant factors related to the different points of view. Central were beliefs about the definition of human life and the relation of human life to the concept of the soul and its infusion.[27]

Legislation accompanied this push for abortion. Three states—California, Colorado, and North Carolina—liberalized their abortion laws in 1967. In 1970, four more states—Hawaii, Alaska, Washington, and New York—enacted abortion-on-demand legislation. New York's laws were the most liberal, allowing for abortion up to twenty-four weeks after conception, and New York City quickly became the abortion capitol of the United States. Whereas in 1966, only 8,000 legal abortions were recorded in this country, 400,000 were estimated to have taken place in 1971.[28]

A reaction began to set in against these liberalized abortion laws and, as a result, the New York legislature reversed its position. However, Governor Nelson Rockefeller vetoed that change. In 1972, abortion laws were on the ballot in Michigan and North Dakota. Everyone was waiting anxiously to see the results of the vote. To the chagrin of the proabortionists, the proposals were overwhelmingly defeated in both states.

Only two months later, in January 1973, the United States Supreme Court did by fiat what could not be accomplished wholly through the legislatures: it established abortion as a constitutional right.[29]

THE CHURCH DIVIDED

In the face of this massive change for abortion, what was the response of the American Christian community? The Roman Catholic Church stood firmly against abortion, and the bishops of New York State sent out a pastoral letter that read, "Laws which allow abortion violate the unborn child's God-given right to life." It pointed out further that the liberalization of abortion laws would invite a "new slaughter of the innocents." How wise they were.[30]

In contrast, Protestants stood in disarray. The American Baptist Convention in 1968 adopted a resolution stating that "abortion should be a matter of responsible personal decision." The United Presbyterian Church, the United Methodist Church, and the Protestant Episcopal Church followed with similar resolutions. Even the Southern Baptist Convention was caught up in the prochoice arguments in 1971, a position it later reversed in 1980.

The Presbyterian Church of the United States adopted a position paper calling for "free choice" in the area of abortion. Such a statement was particularly "progressive" since the Supreme Court had not yet made its decision and since every state in which this denomination had churches still had restrictive abortion codes in effect. In its position paper, the question of fetal humanity or the presence of the image of God in the unborn was not even addressed.[31]

Individual religious leaders spoke out for abortion. Dr. John C. Bennett, president emeritus of Union Theological Seminary in New York, warned against "the invoking of one law or principle in isolation and without regard for the human circumstances." He called the Roman Catholic stand against abortion "an harsh and unconvincing form of legalism."[32] From another realm of Judeo-Christendom, Murray Gordon, chairman of the New York Council of the American Jewish Congress, declared: "The time has come to bring the law in line with social reality." Supporting the liberalization of abortion laws is "a matter of good medicine, good sense, and simple humanity."[33]

And how did the evangelical community react? The response came slowly and was anything but unanimous. A few leaders spoke out clearly against abortion. But many were swayed by the arguments for abortion reform at that time.[34]

THE ROOTS OF CONFLICT

Why was it that the Christian community did not respond in a unified fashion as the early church had? Why did there develop a hesitancy to speak out on behalf of the unborn? Perhaps the answer lies in the deeper conflict taking place in the arenas of philosophy and ethics.

The 1960s in particular was a period of social and moral upheaval, with the assassinations of President Kennedy and Martin Luther King, the mounting death toll in Vietnam, international terrorism, and urban unrest. The "younger generation" experienced a sense of aimlessness and lack of purpose in life. Rising immorality on college campuses and widespread dissemination of birth-control pills for the purpose of controlling reproductive destinies became very evident.

But all these problems were mere symptoms of a society in deeper conflict—a conflict over ideas. Most movements begin not in the details of legal documents or external protests. They begin in the quiet rooms of scholars and in journals and classrooms where ideas are presented. These ideas then generate their logical outcome in social conduct.

Some of the more influential ideas of that decade remind us of ancient Greece. First, there was the stress on "individual freedom," defined primarily as "doing one's own thing." This cry for freedom said, "If it feels good, do it." "If it is right for you, then it is right."

Ethics involves the matter of authority, of choosing who is to decide what is right or wrong. The 1960s was a time when young people, in rebellion, were choosing to be their own authorities.

This stress on being free from all authority outside oneself was bolstered by existentialism and situation ethics. Existentialism assumes there are no moral absolutes and that there is no inherent worth in the self, no pre-established value of man. Man becomes valuable through his or her own choices. The authentic person is one who is free to make his own decisions, and unless one is free to do so, he is not fully human. Hence, being free from all authority outside oneself is crucial.

Similarly, situation ethics leaves the choice of what is right primarily up to the individual. Joseph Fletcher, who popularized this approach, says there is one main ethical principle, the law of love. In any situation, a person must do what love demands. But how does one determine what love demands in a given situation? While Fletcher tries to provide a number of guidelines for doing this, the final norm rests on the individual who is in the process of choosing. Fletcher rejects the idea of any absolute authority outside oneself.

At the root of this rapid change in moral opinion was the rejection of an absolute moral authority. In the churches this involved the rejection of God and his Word. In seminaries, the "God is dead" movement sprang up; God was not needed any more. Skeptical views of Scripture and its authority dominated mainline denominations.

Slowly but steadily, the belief that man is the center of the universe replaced reliance upon God. Man had again come of age in a "new enlightenment." A fresh awareness of the potential for man to determine his own destiny was the creative force behind the changing morals of that time. We were encouraged to think of ourselves as living in a post-Christian era in which freedom and self-determination held sway rather than any "sectarian" or authoritarian dogma.

The *Humanist Manifesto II*, written in 1973, plainly declared there was no God and no place for prayer or piety in modern society. It affirmed that "moral values derive their source from human experience. Ethics is autonomous and situational, needing no religious or ideological sanction."[35]

The *Manifesto* also declared "the right to abortion" as a basic right, along with the rights of divorce, suicide, euthanasia, and homosexual practice.

All of these philosophical influences (and more) merged into what some have referred to as the "new ethic" among many medical professionals. This new ethic abandoned the longstanding Judeo-Christian consensus and adopted instead what has been called a "quality of life" ethic in which personhood is defined according to the freedom demanded by the times. A distinction similar to Aristotle's formed and unformed fetus emerged—"biological life" and "personhood"—which supported the taking of unborn life. This distinction has had a profound effect on those participating in the abortion debate, as we shall see in the next two chapters.

It was in the midst of this philosophical revolution that the American Law Institute in 1962 first called for "abortion reform."

Of course, Christians are for reform if something needs reforming. But it is often difficult to discern these matters. Scripture compliments the sons of Issachar who came to make David king in Hebron by saying that they were "men who understood the times, with knowledge of what Israel should do" (1 Chronicles 12:32).

Do we understand our times? Do we know what God's people today should do? We will attempt to answer both these questions as we explore in this book the critical issue of abortion.

Chapter 1, Notes

1. The origin of this old Latin hymn is unknown. It was translated by Francis Pott and is known by its first line, "The strife is o'er, the battle done."

2. "Beyond 1984: An Evangelical Agenda," *Christianity Today*, 18 January 1985, 16.

3. Franky Schaeffer, "Sincere People: How Evangelical Leaders Have Capitulated to the Abortion Industry," *The Christian Activist*, Winter 1985, 1.

4. Abortion was mentioned as early as the second millennium B.C.—in a negative way. Assyrian law penalized self-induced abortion by prescribing death by torture. The text reads: "If a woman by her own deed has cast that which is within her womb, and a charge has been brought and proved against her, they shall impale her and not bury her. If she dies from casting that which is in her womb, they shall impale her and not bury her." Cf. James B. Pritchard, *Ancient Near Eastern Texts Relating to the Old Testament* (Princeton: Princeton University Press, 1950), 184.

5. Plato *Republic* 5.9.

6. Aristotle *Historia animalium* 7.3; see also his *Politics* 7.1.1, 7.14.10.

7. Michael J. Gorman, *Abortion and the Early Church* (Downers Grove, Ill.: InterVarsity Press, 1982), 25. Gorman's work is well documented and considers in depth what we are briefly pointing to in our introduction. For a brief survey of the same time period by someone who is prochoice, see Martin J. Buss, "The Beginning of Human Life as an Ethical Problem," *Journal of Religion* 47 (July 1967):244-55.

8. Gorman, *Abortion*, 48.

9. The case for *pharmakeia* implying abortion in Galatians 5:19- 21 may be summarized this way. The root *pharmakon* is found in several such New Testament lists. Revelation 9:21 reads, "and they did not repent of their murders nor of their sorceries (*pharmakon*) nor of their immorality nor of their thefts." Sorcerers (*pharmakoi*) along with murderers, immoral persons, and idolaters are assigned to the lake that burns with fire and brimstone (Revelation 21:8), and are outside the New Jerusalem (22:15).

These New Testament references would mean little were it not for two of the earliest Christian sources available, written at the turn of the first century. Both the Didache and the Epistle of Barnabas condemn abortion in contexts very similar to Galatians and Revelation. The Didache (A.D. 70-110) contrasts two lifestyles—the way of life and the way of death. Concerning the way of life, it declares: "Thou shalt not murder a child by abortion/destruction." Barnabas (A.D. 100-130) makes basically the same statement. In both documents, the context is two-fold. First, the condemnation is accompanied by a list of prohibitions such as murder, immorality, and the like. Second, it is included in an exposition of the second commandment of our Lord, "You shall love your neighbor as yourself." This is the precise context of *pharmakeia* in Galatians 5.

10. For documentation, see Gorman, *Abortion*, 47-73.

11. "The Twelve Apostles," in the Epistle of Barnabas, 19:5; see *Doctrina duodecum apostolorum; Barnabae epistula*, ed. Theodor Klauser (Bonn, 1940); cited in the *Christian Action Council Resource Manual*, SM-13.

12. *Sermons*, i, 12; cited in the *Christian Action Council Resource Manual*, SM-14.

13. *Pedagogus*, ii, 10:95-96; cited in the *Christian Action Council Resource Manual*, SM-14.

14. Athenagoras *Legatio* 35; in *The Ante-Nicene Fathers*, ed. Alexander Roberts and James Donaldson, 10 vols. (Grand Rapids: Wm. B. Eerdmans Publishing Co., 1951-1953). The visionary Apocalypse of Peter (ca. A.D. 100) paints this awful scene of hell, depicting the writer's strong feelings on the subject of abortion: "And near that place I saw another gorge in which the discharge and excrement of the tortured ran down and became like a lake. And there sat women, and the discharge came up to their throats; and opposite them sat many children, who were born prematurely, weeping. And from them sent forth rays of fire and smote the women on the eyes. And these were those who produced children outside marriage and who procured abortions." Cf. Apocalypse of Peter, 26, the Akhmim Fragment, in Edgar Hennecke, *New Testament Apocrypha*, ed. Wilhelm Schneemelcher, English ed. R. McL. Wilson (Philadelphia: Westminster Press, 1963-1965), 2:674.

15. Gorman, *Abortion*, 20-21, 33-45. For Jewish views in the first century, see the article by Rabbi Immanuel Jacobovits, "Jewish Views on Abortion," *Human Life Review* I.1 (Winter 1975).

16. *Contra Julianum*, v, 34 (ch. 8), P.L., xliv, 804-5. Augustine believed that handicapped children are formed by God: "For he is born feeble minded by an accidental defect, but he is created as a man by the work of God" (*Operus imperfecti contra Julianum*, iii, 160-1; P.L., xlv, 1313-1315). He also believed that a child is born in the uterus before being born outside of the mother (*Erarratio in almum*, lxii, P.L., xxxvi, 678), and argued that the fetus is not part of the mother (*Contra Julianum*, vi, 43 (ch. 14); P.L., xliv, 847). All of these references are cited in the *Christian Action Council Resource Manual*, SM-15.

17. *Summa Theologicae*, iii, qu. 668, art. 11. Aquinas thought the unborn was wholly distinct from the mother as soon as it acquired a soul; but there was no spiritual soul in an unformed embryo. He also thought the unborn "live with" God and are sanctified by him. Cf. the *Christian Action Council Resource Manual*, SM-15.

18. Karl Barth wrote: "The unborn child is from the very first a child. It is still developing and has no independent life. But it is a man and not a thing, nor a mere part of the mother's body. . . . He who destroys germinating life kills a man." (Barth, *Church Dogmatics*, English ed. G. W. Bromiley and T. F. Torrance [Edinburgh: T. & T. Clark, 1961], vol. 3, *The Doctrine of Creation*, 415ff.) Emil Brunner, *The Divine Imperative*, trans. Olive Wyon (Philadelphia: Westminster, 1947), 367ff. Dietrich Bonhoeffer wrote in *Ethics*, trans. Neville Horton Smith (New York: Macmillan, 1955), 131: "The simple fact is that God intended to create a human being and that this human being has been deliberately deprived of his life. And that is nothing but murder." Helmut Thielicke, *The Ethics of Sex* (New York: Harper, 1964), 227-28.

19. Victor G. Rosenblum, *Abortion, Personhood and the Fourteenth Amendment* (Chicago: Americans United For Life, Inc., 1981).

20. *Roe v.Wade*, 410 U.S. 113 (1973), Section VI, Nos. 1, 2 (pp. 130-2).

21. H. O. J. Brown, "What The Court Didn't Know," *Human Life Review*, I.2 (Spring 1975), 5.

22. Philosopher Arthur F. Holmes in his book, *Ethics: Approaching Moral Decisions* (Downers Grove, Ill.: InterVarsity Press, 1984), 9, summarizes the sixties in this way: "In the 1960s a moral revolution that had been brewing for decades burst upon us. Some of it was highly commendable, especially the

refusal to accept abuses of political, economic and military power. But in rejecting establishment ways it also changed accepted sexual morality, it took individualism to narcissistic extremes, and it placed in jeopardy existing ideals for marriage and family, work and government. This in turn has produced conservative reactions that polarize us both morally and politically over issues like human rights, criminal punishment and legislating morality, as well as sex and war."

23. Cf. Thomas F. Lambert, "The Legal Rights of the Fetus," in *Birth Control and the Christian*, ed. Spitzer and Saylor (Wheaton: Tyndale House, 1969), 402-4.

24. Ibid., 404. In 1859, the AMA unanimously adopted the following anti-abortion resolution condemning "the procuring of abortion, at every period of gestation, except as necessary for preserving the life of either mother or child," and requesting "the zealous cooperation of the various state medical societies in pressing this subject upon the legislatures of the respective states" (Horatio Storer, *Criminal Abortion in America* [Philadelphia: Lippincott, 1860], 99f.). By 1971, the AMA endorsed abortion when it serves "the best interests of the patient" (Cf. *Roe* v. *Wade*, 410 U.S. 113 (1973), p. 143).

25. Cf. Lambert, "Legal Rights," 408-10; also, Christopher T. Reilly, "Threatened Health of Mother as an Indication for Therapeutic Abortion," *Birth Control and the Christian*, ed. Spitzer and Saylor (Wheaton: Tyndale House, 1969), 173-76. Part of the 1968 ACOG policy statement reads: "Therapeutic abortion may be performed for the following established medical indications:

> 1) When continuation of the pregnancy may threaten the life of the woman or seriously impair her health. In determining whether or not there is such a risk to health, account may be taken of the patient's total environment, actual or reasonably foreseeable. 2) When pregnancy has resulted from rape or incest: in this case the same medical criteria should be employed in the evaluation of the patient. 3) When continuation of the pregnancy would result in the birth of a child with grave physical deformities or mental retardation."

26. John T. Noonan, Jr., *A Private Choice: Abortion in America in the Seventies* (New York: Free Press, 1979), 36f.

27. For further results of the three polls respectively, cf. *Eternity*, February 1971, 21; *Birth Control and the Christian*, ed. Spitzer and Saylor (Wheaton: Tyndale House, 1969), 173; John Warwick Montgomery, *Slaughter of the Innocents* (Westchester, Ill.: Crossway Books, 1981), 76.

28. Cf. Lambert, "Legal Rights," 404-8; Harold O. J. Brown, *Death Before Life* (Nashville: Thomas Nelson Publishing House, 1977), 73-74.

29. *Roe* v. *Wade* and *Doe* v. *Bolton* were the twin decisions that brought this about. Cf. Brown, *Death Before Life*, 73-96, for an overview of the Supreme Court's decision.

30. *Christianity Today*, 28 April 1967, 43.

31. Cf. Thomas Warren's comments on the 1970 position paper adopted by the PCUS, in *Presbyterian Survey*, May 1981, 9.

32. *Christianity Today*, 28 April 1967, 43.

33. Ibid.

34. The evangelical response is developed in chapter three.

35. *Humanist Manifesto II* first appeared in *The Humanist*, September-October 1973. The introduction and the first and third statements in the manifesto should be read.

Chapter 2

What Is a Person?

"*I*f every human fetal organism is a person, and if we think it is immoral to end such forms of human life unnecessarily . . . we will logically look upon abortion at will as immoral," writes Joseph Fletcher, author of the well-known book, *Situation Ethics*. "If, on the other hand, we do not regard uterine life as human in the sense of a personal being we will not believe its termination is 'murder.'. . ."[1]

What is a person? It seems an easy question, and perhaps it was, once upon a time. But today, in the midst of numerous quandaries in bioethics, the answer seems to be up for grabs. As Joseph Fletcher, a major proponent of abortion, summarizes in the quote above, personhood is the crux of the matter. Everything in the abortion debate hinges on whether or not the unborn are viewed as persons.

This is not to say that personhood is the only issue raised in a discussion of abortion. Prochoice advocates argue that we need to protect the woman's freedom of choice and that the government should not interfere with her right to privacy. They cite the need to control the world's population growth and to battle poverty. They speak of the physical and emotional burden the handicapped place on their families and society.

All these rationales for abortion are to some degree credible. They seem humane. But if a fetus is a person, these arguments appear in quite a different light. Does freedom of choice include the choice of killing a person? Does the woman have a right to a private decision about her future and that of her fetus if in fact that fetus is another person in the womb? Can social policies for controlling population growth or curbing poverty include the killing of those now living? Obviously, if we regard the unborn as persons, we would answer these questions no, no, and no! Persons have rights.

And so we return to the central question. What is a person?

When the movement toward legalized abortion began in the 1960s, it did not have to face the issue of personhood in the same way it does now. The general public did not know just how human the fetus was—how soon the heart beat, the hands formed, the brain waves began pulsing. The way in which the prochoice camp defended its position was primarily to talk of the fetus in terms of a blob, a mass of tissue, or a parasite. These terms dehumanized the unborn, but as they are no longer convincing, new arguments are being put forth.

The main spokespersons for abortion are no longer trying to deny the humanity of the unborn. Virtually all agree that "human life" begins at conception (a few try to argue otherwise, but without force). Instead they are making a new and crucial distinction between human life and a human being—that is, between biological life and personhood. Joseph Fletcher insists that we cannot begin to understand the abortion issue until we are able to make this distinction. For him, it is impermissible to use the terms human *life* and *person* interchangeably: "Not to know what we mean by these terms is simply to flounder around when we talk about moral decisions."[2]

The result of this distinction is to make a separation between that which has biological life but is not yet in the full sense a person, and that which is judged to have arrived at full personhood. As Richard John Neuhaus, Lutheran pastor and author, observes: "Wherever we find ourselves in the abortion debate, it is past time to recognize that we are in painful fact deciding who is and who is not a human being entitled to societal protection."[3]

When the Supreme Court said in the landmark *Roe* v. *Wade* decision in 1973 that the law need not protect those who are not "persons in the whole sense," they made this distinction to exclude the unborn from protection against abortion. For in constitutional law, a person is an entity entitled to rights and equal protection under the law.

As a technical legal term, *person* has been used in courts to protect human beings, a body of individuals, and even corporations. On the other hand, if certain "entities" such as unborn children, handicapped infants, or the elderly senile can be classified by law as nonpersons, then those same courts can dismiss any rights they might have to equal protection under law. This is what the argument surrounding personhood is all about.

QUALITY OF LIFE

Let's assume the prochoice premise that not everything that is genetically *Homo sapiens* is really a person. How then would one qualify as a person in the full sense of the word? How and when would biological human life be considered by society to be an individual with human rights? There would have to be criteria, standards to go by. In today's parlance, they are called "quality of life" criteria.

Differences of opinion exist among prochoice thinkers as to what these criteria are and how much development is required for personhood to be achieved. Just what is the essential element, the *sine qua non*, without which there is no person? The possibilities can be grouped into several categories: physical, social, and mental standards.

Physical Criteria

There are two types of physical criteria offered as solutions for determining actual personhood. The first is based on time, and holds that life is not fully human until a certain stage of physical development is reached.

Glanville Williams of Cambridge University, for example, is inclined to think that viability—ability to survive outside the womb—is the beginning point of personhood.[4] Ethicist N. J. Berrill contends that personhood begins when all the organs are present in rudimentary form, some time between the sixth and eighth weeks of development.[5] Others point to the beginning of blood circulation, the movement of brain waves, or the taking of the first breath.

A second physical criterion centers around the health of a person; forty-six chromosomes must be present in each cell, developing normally, to qualify for personhood. Birth defects supposedly render an organism unable to live a meaningful life, and place too much of a burden on society. Ethicist James Gustafson of the University of Chicago writes, "Respect for life does not necessarily indicate the preservation of human physical life at the cost of unbearable pain to individuals, and even to families around them."[6]

Nobel Prize winning biologist Francis Crick argues that we should wait until children are at least two days old before we legally declare them persons; by that time we will be able to certify that they are healthy.[7] A belief in eugenics seems to lie behind this intense concern for the physical side of man—a conviction that the realization of humanity and good health are identical. Quality of life is defined within the quest for a perfect world inhabited only by perfect people, free from the burdens of physical deformities and genetic diseases.

Social Criteria

A second group bases quality of life on social criteria, believing that interaction with other human beings on a nonbiological level is necessary in order for one to be a person. They look for capacities such as love, self-consciousness, and the ability to relate and communicate with others. If a child has not reached a certain maturity in such relationships, then that child is not yet a person.

Ashley Montague, a British anthropologist and a prolific

writer, argues that a baby does not become human until he is molded by social and cultural influences. So then, a Ph.D. is more human than a two-year-old. Man's cultural accomplishments—what he does and makes—set him apart from the animal world.[8]

Joshua Lederberg, a leading geneticist, believes we should consider an infant's intellectual development, acquisition of language, and ability to participate in a "meaningful, cognitive interaction with his mother and with the rest of society." Only at this point has the "infant" achieved those attributes that set him apart from the rest of the animal world.[9]

For philosopher Michael Tooley, an individual who has a right to life must be someone who is consciously aware of his continuing existence and is free to desire its continuance. This conscious awareness and desire for life's continuance are the properties needed for one to become a person. Tooley concludes negatively that "a newborn baby does not possess the concept of a continuing self, any more than a newborn kitten possesses such a concept."[10] Therefore, infanticide is morally permissible.

Tooley's view creates a dilemma that, strangely enough, concerns adult animals such as "cats, dogs, polar bears."[11] Might they not also possess properties that endow them with a right to life? For if we say that a person is one who possesses a consciousness of a continuing self, might not these animals fit into that category? We may have to conclude, says Tooley, that our everyday treatment of animals is "morally indefensible," and when we dispose of them we are in fact "murdering innocent persons."[12]

Mental Criteria

Most popular as a barometer of quality of life is mental ability. Many scholars hold that man is distinct from animal life primarily because of intelligence. Consequently, unless the individual demonstrates some degree of reason, volition, or self-awareness, he or she is not a human being.

Author Rudolph Ehrensing, noting that cessation of brain activity is a commonly accepted sign of death, holds that commencement of brain activity should therefore be the first sign of human life.[13] Another scholar, Roy Schenk, argues that the cerebral cortex must develop to a level of self-awareness before the fetus becomes an actual person. For him, this point probably does not occur before the sixth month of pregnancy.[14]

Joseph Fletcher goes even further and says that an individual is not a person unless he has an I.Q. of at least 40 on the Stanford-Binet intelligence scale.[15] Obviously, a fetus or newborn child cannot even take the test and therefore does not qualify. On the other end of the spectrum, the elderly may become so senile they could score in this low range. In such cases, says Fletcher, abortion, infanticide, and euthanasia are not the taking of personal life, merely of biological life.

The mental criteria view actually holds, when consistent, that a chimpanzee can be more human than a mentally handicapped baby. The important thing is the mental capacity and size of the brain. If a child is born with Down's syndrome or spina bifida with hydrocephalus, his brain will never develop sufficiently for him to be a person, according to some. Philosopher Peter Singer of the Centre for Human Bioethics writes:

> If we compare a severely defective human infant with a nonhuman animal, a dog or a pig, for example, we will often find the nonhuman to have superior capacities, both actual and potential, for rationality, self-consciousness, communication, and anything else that can plausibly be considered morally significant.[16]

Winston L. Duke, a nuclear physicist, argues that the same is even true of a perfectly normal infant: "it should be recognized that not all men are human. . . . It would seem to be more inhumane to kill an adult chimpanzee than a newborn baby, since the chimpanzee has greater mental awareness."[17]

Combining Criteria

As you might expect, many in the prochoice camp determine quality of life not from a single criterion but from a combination of physical, mental, and social criteria. An excellent example of this approach is Mary Anne Warren, a professor at Sonoma State College in California, who lists what are to her the "most essential traits" of personhood:

> 1) consciousness (of objects and events external and/
> or internal to the being), and in particular the capac-
> ity to feel pain;
> 2) reasoning (the *developed* capacity to solve new
> and relatively complex problems);
> 3) self-motivated activity (activity which is rela-
> tively independent of either genetic or direct external
> control);
> 4) the capacity to communicate, by whatever means,
> messages of an indefinite number of possible con-
> tents, but on indefinitively many possible topics;
> 5) the presence of self-concepts, and self-awareness,
> either individual or racial, or both. [18]

Warren qualifies her own list in several ways. She calls it a "very rough" list and admits that "there are apt to be a great many problems involved in formulating precise definitions of these criteria." Then she adds three more qualifications: (1) Not all five criteria are needed, perhaps one or two alone may be sufficient. (2) We should not insist that any one of these criteria are "necessary" for personhood, although again the first three are the most important. However, (3) any individual who does not satisfy any of the five criteria is certainly not a person.

Shifting Standards

Up to this point, I have recorded prochoice apologists' criteria without comment. But two comments are worth mentioning here. First, Warren seems uncertain about her list. Second, her list draws our attention by its apparent arbitrary nature. She requires "a developed capacity to solve new and relatively complex problems," and a capacity to communicate "not just with an indefinite number of possible contents, but on indefinitely many possible topics." How Warren came up with these criteria would be an interesting question.

One thing is obvious about Warren's and the others' efforts to define personhood by quality of life: Quality of life is an arbitrary standard. There is no agreement as to its definition. One scholar says this, another says that. When some of the criteria are examined closely (e.g. the ability to love), we find them to be nebulous and impossible to measure.

Prochoice advocates also disagree about the time element of achieving personhood. Some believe the fetus becomes a person at a late point in pregnancy. Others—a growing number—have chosen a point at birth or some time after.

Thomas L. Hayes, a biophysicist at Berkeley, thinks that as development proceeds, so does life's value. "The human individual develops biologically in a continuous fashion, and . . . the rights of a human person might develop in a similar way."[19] At what point, one wonders, might the rights of the fetus equal those of the mother?

A similar sentiment is held by Norman Gillespie:

> Given our awareness of the spectrum of poverty to riches, from baldness to a full head of hair, and from conception to adulthood, we can specify quite precisely where an individual falls along any of those spectrums. So precision is possible without drawing any lines and in determining the rights of a being we can proceed in exactly the same fashion. Thus, when an adult requests an abortion, if it is seen as a conflict of rights case, the comparative strength of the rights of the being to be aborted is determined by its stage and development.[20]

While Gillespie says precision is possible (without drawing lines!), he gives us no clue as to exactly how comparisons should be made. The decision is left to the arbitrary whims of the decider.

PROCHOICE LOGIC

Understanding the various criteria for personhood is central, but it is only the beginning. We must also understand the logic behind these criteria.

The scholars I quote and summarize in the following section are concerned for what is morally right, but they also appear to be searching for some way to justify abortion. It would be hard, if not impossible, to live with yourself if you knew you were responsible for killing innocent people. But these prochoice advocates seem to believe they are not killing people. According to their logic, the unborn are nonpersons, merely "potential" persons in the process of developing to persons in the full sense of that term. When you read their arguments, you will see they have different nuances, but are at root the same.

Lederberg: Logic of Process vs. Event

In a speech given in 1967, Professor Joshua Lederberg, Ph.D. in genetics and presently head of the Rockefeller Institute, linked "quality of life" logic with the logic of evolution.[21] To paraphrase his words, when people raise the question, "When does life begin?" they do so with a predetermined answer in mind. "When" implies a point in time. But in fact, all our basic knowledge about biology, evolution, and development processes *opposes setting a specific point in time* as the beginning of an individual human life. The only point in time was an event that occurred some three billion years ago when life began. Moreover, there is no absolute right to life for the unborn, for the fertilized egg is not unique when compared to other tissues. Very little differentiates the human DNA from that of the ape, monkey, or other primate species.

The best we can do is compare fetal development with the evolutionary development of the species. In the latter, there was "no sudden emergence of human personality," but rather "the gradual accumulation of those genetic alterations controlling the development of the brain that in turn permit the development of humanity."

Likewise, the fetus undergoes that same process. At first, the fetus is no nearer to being a human being than is an unborn ape or chick. Even the newborn infant must develop further to achieve full humanity:

> An operationally useful point of divergence of the developing organism would be at approximately the first year of life, when the human infant continues his intellectual development, proceeds to the acquisition of language, and then participates in a meaningful, cognitive interaction with his mother and with the rest of society. At this point only does he enter into the cultural tradition that has been the special attribute of man by which he is set apart from the rest of the species.

What Lederberg is saying is this: Conception is a process and not a special event. A fertilized egg begins on par with the animals. A period of time is necessary to "achieve" complete humanity. Our problem then is a pragmatic one—to choose a point in time at which a child is set apart from animal species. For Lederberg, that point is one year of age and his criteria center around the intellect and social relationships.

Clearly, this would allow for infanticide. Lederberg pleads that we cannot let our emotions regarding infants interfere with "objective biological standards" for establishing reasonable laws. Sustaining the handicapped merely delays the elimination of those "deleterious mutations" through natural selection. While we must develop constructive methods to avoid handicaps through contraception and genetic control of fertility, we *need* abortion when a "grossly impaired infant" is anticipated. It is not a person—it has not gone through the necessary process.

Hardin: The Logic of Potential vs. Actual

Garrett Hardin is professor of biology at the University of California in Santa Barbara. Writing in 1967 before abortion was legalized, Hardin joins Lederberg as one of the early proponents for the repeal of abortion laws. He asks, "Is abortion murder?" and answers, Whether the fetus is or is not a human being is a matter of definition, not fact; and "we are free to define it any way we like."

Hardin reasons that the killing of "very young embryos" is different from killing at another stage in life. We are not the same person at different stages of life. For example, no one would mistake an embryo for an adult, not even for a three-year-old child. In fact, no one could recognize with the naked eye a three-week-old embryo as a human being. "Is it right, then, to say that John Smith at twenty-one days of true age is in some sense identical with John Smith at 7,938 days? Potentially, the former can develop into the latter. But is this *potential* important or valuable enough to justify damaging the unwilling mother's life by refusing to sacrifice the potential?" (italics his).[22]

Human development begins with a fertilized egg. Structurally there is no resemblance to a human being. Materially it is virtually indistinguishable from the living material of any other animal cell. However, within this cell is a tiny substance called DNA which is a "blueprint" for becoming a human being. Says Hardin, "The weight of this DNA is fantastically small—only 6 picograms. To put this in homely perspective: if all the DNA of all the fertilized eggs that produced the world's present population [in 1967] of 3,500,000,000 people had been gathered together in one lump, it would have weighed only one-third as much as one postage stamp. Yet this tiny amount of DNA contained the directions for producing all the people of the world."

Is this DNA precious, since it has all this potential? No! says Hardin. It is only a blueprint, and the blueprint is not the real thing. The DNA of a zygote is not a human being. Clearly then, "all life is not equally valuable." The equation, life (of 10 days) = life (of 8,000 days) is not true.

Of course as development proceeds, value accrues since the blueprints are gradually realized in the structure of *homo sapiens*. But there is no sharp line that tells us at which point life becomes objectively valuable. We may have to draw an arbitrary line to which society can agree, possibly at twelve weeks of pregnancy.

Hardin's logic parallels that of Lederberg. Both are premised on the idea of development. But whereas Lederberg focuses on "process," Hardin focuses on the concept of "potential."

Charles Hartshorne: Genes and Personhood

We need not stay with those in the secular setting to find staunch defenders of abortion. Sometimes the loudest proponents, such as Dr. Charles Hartshorne of the University of Texas, Austin, wear a Christian label. The presuppositions of all our previous prochoice advocates are found in his article, "Concerning Abortion: An Attempt at a Rational View."[23]

Proceeding in dialectic style, Hartshorne says: "We are told that the fetus is alive and that therefore killing it is wrong." Mosquitoes, bacteria, apes, whales, and even plants are also alive. However, says the antiabortionist, plants and whales and the like are not human; the fetus is. Aha! retorts Hartshorne, in what sense is the fetus human? That is the issue! "Granted that a fetus is human in origin and possible destiny, in what further sense is it human? The entire problem lies here. If there are prolife activists who have thrown much light on this question, I do not know their names."

A fertilized egg is only a single cell and cannot be thought of as an actual person. "It cannot speak, reason or judge between right and wrong. It cannot have personal relations, without which a person is not *functionally* a person at all, until months—and not, except minimally, until years—have passed" (italics mine).

These are the qualities that prove our superior worth to chimpanzees or dolphins. The "egg cell" or "colony of cells" in early development cannot even be compared to an individual animal that has progressed beyond that point. The only thing we can state positively about a fetus at this stage of development is that it is a "possible individual person," or that its "probable destiny" is as an individual person. But it is not an *actual* person!

What about the soul? asks Hartshorne. Can we not say that the fertilized egg already has a human soul? On what evidence? The only relevant evidence is "the capacity to reason, judge right and wrong, and the like." Obviously, a fertilized egg fails to qualify.

But should not the fact that a new and unique human individual is created at conception with his own combination of genes be a factor? Not according to Hartshorne. Genes may count for inherited traits, but they do not fully determine development:

> From the gene-determined chemistry to a human person is a long, long step. As soon as the nervous system forming in the embryo begins to function as a whole—and not before— the cell colony begins to turn into a *genuinely individual animal*. One may reasonably suppose that this change is accompanied by some extremely primitive individual animal feelings. They cannot be recognizably human feelings, much less human thoughts, and cannot compare with the feelings of a porpoise or chimpanzee in level of consciousness. That much seems as certain as anything about the fetus except its origin and possible destiny (italics mine).

Skipping to a point after birth, Hartshorne concerns himself with the charge that if the fetus is not fully human, neither is the infant. "Of course an infant is not fully human," he says. It cannot speak, reason, or judge right and wrong. It is much closer to being a person than a three-month fetus, for its ability to do these things is progressing. Nevertheless, infanticide is not murder. "Persons who are already *functionally persons in the full sense* have more important rights even than infants" (italics mine).

What about the hopelessly senile? The same holds true for them. If a person is someone who is able to speak, reason, and make moral judgments, then to kill someone who is hopelessly senile or in a permanent coma is not to kill a person. Symbolically, we may have to treat them as such, for there are hazards in not doing so. But they are no longer persons.

Hartshorne's logic goes like this: Genetic development is separate from personhood. Genetically, fetuses may be compared to animals such as pigs and chimpanzees. Persons can speak, reason, make moral judgments, and have personal relations. Therefore, to kill those who are unable to function in this way— such as fetuses, infants, or the senile—is not to kill a person.

In Summary: Joseph Fletcher, the Spokesman

The most famous witness for abortion is Joseph Fletcher, known in most circles for his book, *Situation Ethics: The New Morality*.[24] Fletcher is presently on the faculty of the Medical School at the University of Virginia. His high profile in writing and speaking have had a major impact on bioethics, and his thinking summarizes and organizes much of what we have looked at thus far.

The main concern for Fletcher is to discern what constitutes a person. He first clarifies that not everyone who belongs to the human species is a person. Like Hartshorne, he says that a fetus is *merely biological life*, not a person, because it does not have any of those traits we associate with personhood "such as curiosity, affection, self-awareness and self-control, memory, purpose, conscience—none of the distinctive trans-biological indicators of personality."[25]

Like Lederberg, Fletcher stresses the idea of *process*. He quotes Cyril Means to prove his point: "Live human sperm and egg exist before fertilization: all that occurs is that two squads of twenty-three chromosomes each form up a platoon of forty-six, but there is no more human life . . . than there was before."[26] "Life never begins," it is merely passed on by means of conception. In fact, to speak of a moment when life begins, a moment of death, or a moment when anything else biotic "occurs" is inaccurate, biologically speaking.[27]

Like Hardin, Fletcher also stresses the concept of *potentiality*. "The sadness of abortion is that it means letting a potential go, but it is only a potential, not a reality."[28] To say that the potential is the actual "is like saying that an acorn is an oak or a promise is its fulfillment or a blueprint is a house."[29] A fetus is only a potential person and does not become an actual person until it achieves certain standards.

The central issue for Fletcher is his *criteria for personhood*. Fletcher is well aware that one's definition of personhood can become quite arbitrary. For if life is a process and conception is no more significant than any other biological moment, then any one definition of personhood is as good as another.

In an effort *not* to be arbitrary, Fletcher wrote several essays on the criteria for personhood. In his first essay, "Indicators of Humanhood: A Tentative Profile of Man," Fletcher challenged his cohorts to become more specific and concrete in spelling out an actual inventory or profile of man. Fletcher then threw down the gauntlet by listing his own criteria or indicators, and inviting others to critique his list. His list included fifteen positive and five negative propositions to determine if someone were truly a person.[30]

In a second essay written two years later (and apparently after a great deal of discussion on the issue), the twenty criteria had been reduced to four traits that make up the essence of humanhood: neocortical function, self-consciousness, relational ability, and happiness.[31] Though Fletcher now identified four traits of humanhood, the cerebral cortex was for him the *sine qua non* of personhood. For without the cerebral cortex, the other three cannot function.

In a book written in 1974 (about the same time as the essay mentioned above), Fletcher argued that only two essential qualities are necessary in order for a human being to be classified as a person: some "minimal level of intelligence," and "individual or separate existence."[32]

As one examines all Fletcher's literature, it becomes apparent that everything depends ultimately on mental capability. Fletcher believes the essence of a person lies in his rational function, "the ratio." In his words: "Before cerebration comes into play, or when it is ended, in the absence of the synthesizing or *thinking* function of the cerebral cortex, the person is nonexistent—or, put another way, the life which is functioning biologically is a nonperson."[33]

In clearer words, a human life that has not developed to a point of thinking rationally, or a human life that has passed that point and is now senile, is not to be treated as a person. Elsewhere Fletcher writes: "The point is that abortion and 'brain death' terminations are biocide, not homocide. All talk of 'killing a human being' in such cases is therefore ethically off the track."[34]

Fletcher's next step is to decide, in an arbitrary way, that anyone with an I.Q. less than 20 on the Stanford-Binet scale would not qualify as a person. Anyone below a 40 I.Q. is questionably a person. Fletcher asks, If an ape had the intelligence of a human being and the human being had only the capabilities of an ape, which would be the human being? His answer—the ape![35]

The Big Three

The distinctives of prochoice logic are clear. Though each of our advocates testified on behalf of abortion in his own particular way, the logical premises of all four were the same:

1. Life is a *process*, a continuum. It takes a period of time for a fetus to grow or develop into a human being or person. Most of our witnesses held that conception itself was a process, not an event. This "developmental" or "gradualist" philosophy of life is at the heart of abortion thinking.

2. A fetus is only a *potential* person. Actual person-hood is achieved only after certain quality of life criteria are acquired. Until these criteria are met, all we can say is that an individual is a potential person.

3. As we discuss those qualities of life that make up a person, *biological development* is *irrelevant* to the discussion. For a person is more than genes; there-fore a definition of personhood does not hinge on a stage of biological growth.

ABORTION LOGIC: A SECOND LOOK

The time has come to consider these three assumptions with more depth, along with our response to the various quality of life criteria. We have allowed our witnesses to present their points of view. A brief critique is now in order. (A scriptural approach to these issues is being reserved for a later chapter.)

Process or Event?

Initially, I did not realize that the "moment of conception" was questioned by leading prochoice thinkers. I merely thought that because the point of conception and its significance could be in conflict with their position, they tended either to overlook this fact of science or tried studiously to avoid reference to it. I now understand that many prochoice leaders are ready to challenge the prevailing statements of science regarding conception.

Society is being asked to consider conception solely as a *process* and not as an event or point in time. The underlying assumption, as we have already noted, is that life is a continuum, constantly in the process of development. Life never begins—it is simply passed on by means of conception.

According to Glanville Williams, the ovum and the sperm were alive in the bodies of the respective parents before fertilization took place. Moreover, fertilization itself is a process that may take anywhere from twenty minutes to over two hours to complete. Therefore, what we call the "moment of conception" is an old wives' tale and cannot be held to be a significant point in a person's life. "The argument that life begins with conception is just as unbiological as the old notion that life begins sometime after conception."[36]

This "process of conception" view is crucial because those who propose it clearly wish to deny the significance of conception. They want us to believe that conception is an insignificant point in life, that the zygote and embryonic stages are not important, and that one might as well pick any other time in gestation—or even after birth—as the time when meaningful life begins.

Moreover, the process theory of conception is consistent with the larger complex of ideas which holds that a human life *develops into* a human being or person. Lederberg, Fletcher, Williams, and others depend upon the naturalistic theory of evolution. This is to be expected, since ideas of natural process and development are based on some form of evolution. For example, evolutionist J. Z. Young argues that the first question on the subject of evolution should perhaps be, "Did life originate at all or has it in some sense always existed?"[37]

Believers in nontheistic evolution suppose there is a strict continuity, not discontinuity, between the animal world and man. Man has descended from lower animals by a perfectly natural process controlled by inherent forces; he differs from animals only in degree. Man is more intelligent and the quality of his life is more complex than lower animals.

Assumed here also is a theory of personality development consistent with evolution. Advocates of this theory say it takes time for a personality to develop from a fertilized egg to a whole person. A person is one who can think, believe, will, and have emotions. These are all *acquired* characteristics and are achieved only through a "process of socialization."

Prochoice thinkers base their views on these assumptions, then try to identify at which point in the process the unborn or born child becomes a person. Yet why should it matter how we treat any human being if, ultimately, we are no different from animals?

What might be said for this process view of conception? Obviously, growth is a process and conception takes time. The illustration of conceiving twins demonstrates the complexity of that process—the splitting of the zygote into two individuals occurs somewhere between the seventh and fourteenth day of pregnancy. But there is an end to that process when what existed formerly literally ceases to exist, and a new conceptus has come into being. There is both the process of fertilization and the point at which that process is completed and a new and unique being begins to exist.

This is why a scholar such as Jerome Lejeune, a professor of fundamental genetics in Paris and a pioneer in detecting chromosomal diseases, can testify to a Senate committee: "Life has a very, very long history but each individual has a very neat beginning, the *moment of its conception*"[38] [italics mine]. Such statements are commonplace in medical science. To insist that there is no difference between an egg before and after fertilization is at odds with scientific inquiry.

It seems evident that the process theory of conception is governed not by scientific data but by evolutionary presuppositions that assume life itself is only a process. This philosophy is then forced on scientific facts surrounding conception to make them conform to that point of view.

This idea of process is a vague one, and the hazards it presents are apparent. It is impossible to determine the point we become persons without being arbitrary. Yet the lives of individuals are being taken or spared according to one's view of when that point occurs.[39]

It is with some concern, therefore, that we find certain evangelicals using the term *process* when discussing abortion. Is this proper? For example, an articulate evangelical spokesman, in lectures seeking to clarify life-and-death issues, said it was hardly proper to speak of a moment of conception, since conception was "a process, beginning with the quick passage of the sperm into the cytoplasm of the ovum and extending surely over the first week of cell division."[40] Not only does he use the term *process*, but he extends it over a period much longer than even Fletcher would suggest. By talking about a process without noting that all are agreed that the process ends in a new life having been conceived is to confuse the issue and to aid the abortion cause. Other examples of evangelicals using this term will be found in the next chapter.

My concern is whether Scripture supports a process view of life. If so, the issue is settled. But if Scripture has another view of conception and the value of human life, then the term *process* needs to be challenged. (This will be examined in more detail in chapters 4 and 5.)

Potential or Actual?

When using the term *potential*, prochoicers are not saying the unborn are persons with potential. The unborn are merely "potential persons" who must develop in certain ways to become "actual persons."

Biologically, they argue, the initial human cells bear no resemblance to those of an adult; some degree of development is needed. Physically, new properties or forms constantly present themselves in the first ten weeks of life. Through a process of differentiation, cells become more complex and acquire different functions (liver cells, nerve cells, and the like). It is a relatively continuous process that takes time.

> An examination of potential does not seem to lead to a single point in time when the new individual comes into being. Rather, it suggests again that there may not be such a single point in nature and that instead, the living system exchanges potential for realized form and function in a continuous way.[41]

This then is their interpretation of the biological data. Sociologically, as we have seen, most view personhood as a developed capacity for reasoning, willing, and relating to others. This assumes that human value is an achievement rather than an endowment, and consequently rules out the personhood of those who cannot or have not achieved. Within this philosophy, *potential* becomes the *terminus technicus* for denying a child's value, since he or she has not yet developed these capacities to a sufficient extent.[42]

Another form of argument for potential is that employed by Fletcher and Hardin. A fetus is "only a potential, not a reality." To say that the potential is the actual "is like saying that an acorn is an oak tree or a promise is its fulfillment or a blueprint is a house."[43]

But this is the very point at issue! Their analogies presuppose their point of view. It would be a more accurate analogy to say a "sapling becomes an oak," for a sapling is living and growing like the zygote. An acorn is dormant.

The other analogies are also misplaced. A promise is in the realm of ideas and is only as real as the integrity of the one who promised. The analogy of a blueprint is interesting for it presupposes a mechanistic view of life. First comes the blueprint, then the foundation, then the walls, and finally the house. A blueprint never becomes part of a house, unless it is used to paper the walls. Zygotes, however, contain in themselves all that goes into the maturing of a human being. As John Wilke, a prolife leader, is fond of saying: "In truth we did not come from a single cell. Rather, each of us once was a single cell; and all we have done since then has been to grow up."[44]

Fletcher's view is clearly mechanistic when he writes: "It takes many years to assemble a personality. A newborn baby starts excitingly soon to take on and store away the makings of a person, but even so it takes a long time."[45] Fletcher views life as taking shape like a clock, part by part. A clock is not fully a clock until, part by part, it is completed and is functioning. It is worthless up to that point. Likewise, he would say that a human life is not fully human until all the component parts are fully formed and functioning. However, a human being is more than the sum total of his parts—organs plus muscles plus bones plus brain matter. He or she is a unique individual of worth before God.

What we have here, as ethicist Robert Joyce astutely observes, is a confusion of two kinds of potentiality: "The potency to cause something to come into existence is improperly identified with the potency for this new being to become fully what it is."[46] The sperm and the ovum are not potential life but potential causes of individual human life. They have the potential to cause an individual to come into existence, whereas the zygote has the potential to become what it already in essence is.

In other words, there is no such thing as a potentially living organism. Every living thing is actual, with more or less potentiality. We are dealing with an actual person with potential, not a potential person. The potential of a human conceptus to know and to love God is an actuality a monkey or a rabbit will never possess.

It is not difficult to discern the real hazards of speaking of "potential persons." Such a distinction effectively relaxes the moral prohibition against abortion. Killing potential persons is clearly less objectionable than killing actual persons.

Also, what sense is there in speaking of the rights of potential persons? Value lies not in the potential of something but in the actual possession of it. As someone has noted: "There is no reason to demand that someone who will one day be a person must be treated as one now. For instance, little Johnny has no right to demand that, because he will become Mary's husband someday, she must treat him as her husband now." According to Mary Anne Warren, if a potential person does have any right to life, it would certainly pale in significance to the right of a woman to obtain an abortion "since the rights of any actual person invariably outweigh those of any potential person, whenever the two conflict."[47]

Another major hazard is that this view runs the risk, logically and more increasingly in practice, of furnishing the precedent and authority for infanticide as well as euthanasia. Once we accept its premise that human value is based on achievement, we are open logically to the machinations of social manipulators. No guard exists against the potential misuse of the accepted norm, which may shift in society to fit the self- interests of power groups. Society could define as nonhuman anyone it finds socially useful so to define.

In the past, definitions of humanity have served to exclude women, Jews, Blacks, Asians, and American Indians. Today, by requiring persons to have such functional abilities as reasoning and the art of communication, the retarded, the premature, the comatose, as well as the senile could be classified as nonpersons.[48]

Prochoice thinkers suppose that nature revolves around function, a point that needs to be examined. But from a biblical point of view, an individual is still a person whether or not he can reach his full potential. Those with handicaps who can never achieve certain mental or social functions as well as those who have lost them in old age are still persons. When you hold in your arms a baby with Tay-Sachs disease, you are holding a person. When you care for a grandparent who is senile, you are caring for a person.

Seeing how the term *potential* is being used in prochoice circles, we may wonder about its use by Christian leaders in the abortion context. One evangelical scholar writes: "All we can safely assert is that [the fetus] is, right throughout pregnancy, at least a *potential* human being, and should therefore be treated with all due respect"[49] (italics his). A leading Reformed ethicist who argues strongly against abortion, still says: "The crucial concern here is that we can say with certainty that at any stage of development the fetus is a potential life, a potential human being, with a high level of probability of becoming a human being, if left to nature."[50]

Recent scientific studies show that the unborn begin at a remarkably early stage to show significant signs of achievement, if that is what we are looking for. But this evidence is still irrelevant since it operates on the premise that achievement determines personhood. It will be important to see whether Scripture teaches that an unborn child is a human being from conception or whether his humanity depends upon his achievements (see chapter 5).

Biology and Personhood

Another premise in the prochoice system of logic is that facts of biology have no bearing whatsoever on the definition of personhood. In this view, when human life begins is a biological question; when personhood begins is a religious or moral question. To say, therefore, that a human being with biological life is a person with rights, based solely on biological facts, is an unwarranted leap from science to moral judgment.

This contrasts with the prolife position which views biological development as an important aspect of a person's life. These two positions were set in sharp focus during a Senate subcommittee investigation seeking to define the beginning of human life.

Dr. Leon Rosenberg testified from a proabortion perspective:

> I know of no scientific evidence which bears on the question of when actual human life exists. . . . I believe the notion embodied in the phrase 'actual human life' is not a scientific one, but rather a philosophic and religious one. . . . When does this potential for human life become actual? I do not know. Moreover, I have not been able to find a single piece of *scientific evidence* which helps me with that question.[51]

By adding the word "actual," Rosenberg makes a distinction between biological human life and personhood.

In response, Dr. Alfred M. Bongioanni, professor of pediatrics and obstetrics at the University of Pennsylvania, argued from a strictly genetic position:

> I have learned from my earliest medical education that human life begins at the time of conception. . . . I submit that human life is present throughout this entire sequence from conception to adulthood and that any interruption at any point throughout this time constitutes a termination of human life.[52]

Biologically it is true that human life begins at conception, that the heart begins beating at four weeks, that brain waves are detected by about six weeks, and so on. But Rosenberg says that biology has no bearing on the definition of "actual" human life or personhood.

What might we say in response, apart from Scripture? First, life is more than genetics and a person is more than a physical body. Therefore, a genetic definition of man is incomplete. Conversely, this does not give us the liberty to discard the biological as irrelevant to personhood. To assume that biology has nothing to contribute to man as man is difficult to prove or support.

Even in the secular realms of psychology and medicine, personality is accepted as an organic unity. Studies show that mental states can produce ulcers, kidney troubles, and other diseases. They also show that the body affects the mind; hunger, sickness, and sleeplessness all exact their toll. Glands have a profound effect on emotions, attitude, and behavior.

Since the unity of body and soul is found in both modern science *and* in Scripture,[53] what reason could we have for ignoring the data of biology? Why should proabortionists insist we do so? Could it be that biological facts tend to undermine their position?

It is easy to point out the hazards of ignoring biological data. Without them, the arbitrary norms of the developmental school could run amuck. It is enormously more difficult to measure and evaluate data from psychology, for example, than in the physical area of traditional medicine. Separating personhood from biological life allows more flexibility of defining personhood as mental and social development.

Daniel Callahan warns that we cannot allow society to be held captive by the arbitrary norms of the developmental school:

> When it is a question of human life, there is a need to act in ways that are *not* arbitrary. A fundamental basis of human freedom and security is that human beings will not be subject to arbitrary, shifting definitions of "human."[54]

He goes on to warn against "setting norms which could too easily shift as people's desires or interpretation of social consequences shift."

Different views about humanness will result in different moral perspectives with regard to the senile, the chronically sick, the handicapped, or wards of the state. An elderly father, whose children live far away and who is under the care of a hospital with "quality of life" doctors, could be given a "death with dignity" because he was too ill and forgetful. A child in the womb, due to decisions of a select group, could be determined to be of no value because the father has a history of sickle-cell anemia.

Are my examples far-fetched? I don't think so. By the year 2030, only two wage earners will help support each elderly person on Social Security. (This contrasts with the present ratio of five to one.) Because our nation is now below zero population growth due to abortion and other factors, the elderly will make up a large proportion of our nation, and Social Security will not be able to meet their needs.

What will society do with the elderly? Will there be a strong incentive to define them in a way that will make euthanasia acceptable? To raise this question is not absurd in view of the fact that infanticide is at present a common practice and "living will" bills have been enacted or are pending in all but three states, Kentucky, Pennsylvania, and Michigan.[55]

Such ideas, of course, are alien to the Christian perspective. Christians believe the dignity and sanctity of human life is something conferred by God. As John Perkins, former president and founder of Voice of Calvary Ministries in Mississippi, is so fond of saying, "We do not have to give dignity to anyone. They already have it by the mere fact they are created in God's image." Perkins, of course, is applying this truth to poor people. It applies equally to any human being.[56]

ELITISM: WHO DEFINES WHOM?

We return, now, to an evaluation of the objectivity of quality of life standards for personhood. We have already commented on the arbitrary nature of the selection of criteria. At least two more disturbing features draw our attention.

First, it should be noted that the quality of life criteria is premised on the assumption that *mankind* is the ultimate determiner of what constitutes a human being. From a biblical point of view, I have a problem with that premise.

It should also be noted that it is *adult* human beings who ultimately decide what is to be called human, and they inevitably do so from an adult perspective.

What we are finding in most fields of study—from physiology and biochemistry to psychology and education—is the tendency to make the fully developed individual the measure of all things. Adults can think logically, interact socially, and respond emotionally. They are physically able to exist independently of others. The qualities of beauty and strength and mental capability are held in high regard. So adults make these "qualities" or "achievements" the criteria of personhood. Dr. William Liley, research professor in perinatal physiology at the University of Auckland, New Zealand, observes:

> There has grown up the habit of regarding the fetus and the neo-nate as a poorly functioning adult rather than as a splendidly functioning baby.[57]

This elitist approach has led society to consider fetal form and function (and even newborns) as inferior, whereas in fact they are "remarkably resilient and appropriate for the placental environment in which they live."[58]

It is difficult not to become judgmental of those who would redefine persons using adult quality of life criteria. For the strong are judging the weak, those with high I.Q.s judging those not yet able to take an I.Q. test, and those who are "self-sufficient" judging the dependent. These judges may perceive themselves to be compassionate and good, but their methods could be viewed as totalitarian in the light of their intended results. For nothing is more totalitarian than to define a group of human beings as nonpersons for the purpose of taking their lives.

Robert E. Joyce, chairman of the philosophy department at St. John's University, perceives the situation in just that way:

> Natalism, the superiority of the born over the unborn, has replaced racism and sexism as the chief atrocity of our time. Fallacious thinking is polluting the atmosphere of thought regarding what a person is when he or she begins.[59]

Today, most of us are suspicious of a jury comprised of all white men deciding the guilt or innocence of a black man. We question the value of a panel of men discussing issues pertaining primarily to women. Yet in the abortion issue, we find adults deciding from an adult perspective whether an unborn child is a person.

Is it possible that quality of life definitions are based on what seems valuable to the definer? Perhaps, rather than a criteria of humanness, what we are seeing is a catalog of what society currently values most in people.

Still another disturbing feature of the quality of life school is its tendency to serve selfish motives. In the words of Joseph Fletcher:

> If we adopt a sensible view that a fetus is not a person there is only one reasonable policy, and that is to put an end to compulsory pregnancy. The ethical principle is that pregnancy, when wanted, is a healthy process, pregnancy when not wanted is a disease—in fact, a venereal disease. The truly ethical question is not whether we can justify abortion but whether we can justify compulsory pregnancy. If our ethics is of the humane brand, we will agree that we cannot justify it, and would not want to.[60]

In Fletcher's view, if the mother wants the child, the child's life is of great worth; if not, the child's life is worth nothing—in fact, it is a "venereal disease." How can we view this as anything other than a self-serving statement?[61]

THE END RESULT

We see in society a subtle but momentous shift from the *sanctity of life* position to the *quality of life* position. Archibald Cox, former law professor and Watergate prosecutor, justly criticized the Supreme Court following its decision in 1973:

> The [Court's] opinion fails even to consider what I would suppose to be the most compelling interest of the state in prohibiting abortion: the interest in maintaining that respect for the paramount sanctity of human life which has always been at the center of western civilization.[62]

This quality of life philosophy is being translated today into frightening consequences. One in four pregnancies now end in abortion—that translates into over 1.5 million abortions annually in the United States and 50 to 75 million annually worldwide. Man himself is being consumed as he is redefined by a quality of life ethic.

Yet some Christians seem oblivious to the harm of this shift in philosophy. An eminent biblical scholar, in an article evaluating biogenetic engineering, concludes that "both Christian and non-Christian are slowly coming to the conviction that the *supreme* norm in ethics is the quality of life and not the pure fact of life" (italics mine). Then he makes this astonishing statement, which could have been written by a proabortionist:

> But if we ask: "What is human life intended to be?" perhaps we can get around this highly emotional question. If the goal of life is a mature, rational integrated adult, then we may say that any human life that is way off course and can never reach that goal, can never fulfill what it means to be a complete human person.[63]

Of course, no Christian should be against a high quality of life. This is especially true in regard to the handicapped. This means respecting their identity and needs. We must be *for* them, speaking and acting on their behalf. When Jesus met the man born blind from birth and the paralytic, he did not say, "Because you are physically handicapped, I recommend death as an alternative." He healed them. In the same way, God means for us to respond in love and care and in any way possible to help increase the quality of the lives of those handicapped. He does not want us to take their lives.

Whereas the depth and abundance of one's quality of life may vary widely, it in no way eliminates the sanctity of life. Persons who are profoundly retarded are still people made in God's image. There is no reason to believe that a mother's illness during pregnancy or an extra chromosome or the lack of oxygen during birth could erase that image. As Ronald Greer well remarks:

> They, like us, are finite and imperfect, only their finiteness and imperfection are more obvious and ours more subtle. And they, like us, have been created in the likeness, in the image of God and endowed with the dignity and respect that goes with it.[64]

Rather than setting up criteria that deny personhood to the weak, the unborn, and the deformed, would it not be better to move toward creating a society in which the lives of all people are valued? Instead of destroying life, we should destroy the conditions that make life intolerable.

Jesus said, "I came that they might have life, *and* might have it abundantly." The two positions meet in Jesus' statement. Quality and sanctity of life are not in opposition; neither one cancels out or replaces the other. Yet Christians in recent years— and still today—have reacted with confusion to the abortion issue, as we shall see in our next chapter.

Chapter 2, Notes

1. Joseph Fletcher, *The Ethics of Genetic Control: Ending Reproductive Roulette* (Garden City, N. Y.: Anchor Press, 1974), 134.

2. Ibid., 133. Fletcher is clear about the importance of these distinctions: "Abortion provides a test. Ethically the core issue is whether an embryo or fetus is a human being, and if so in what sense we call it that. How we assess the morality of abortion follows from how we answer this question. . . . There is no argument, of course, about a human fetus being a stage of the species *homo sapiens*; it is easily recognizable biologically. Nor is there any question of its being alive. Cell division is proceeding. But what about claims of personhood or humanhood for a fetus? . . . The nonpersonal view of fetuses fits in with the morality of elective abortion or abortion on request, as well as with therapeutic abortion for medical reasons."

3. Richard John Neuhaus, *The Christian Century*, 29 February 1979, 206.

4. Glanville Williams, "The Legalization of Medical Abortion," *The Eugenics Review* 56 (April 1964): 20-21.

5. N. J. Berrill, *The Person in the Womb* (New York: Dodd, Mead & Co., 1968), 46.

6. James M. Gustafson, *The Contribution of Theology to Medical Ethics* (Milwaukee: Marquette University, 1975), 60.

7. Francis Crick, *Nature* 220 (2 November 1968): 429-30. Cited by Bill Crouse, "Abortion and Human Value," *Insight* (Dallas: Probe Ministries International, 1979), 2.

8. Ashley Montague, *Sex, Man and Society* (New York: G. P. Putnam and Sons, 1967).

9. Joshua Lederberg, "A Geneticist Looks at Contraception and Abortion," *Annals of Internal Medicine* 67 (September 1967): 26f.

10. Michael Tooley, "Abortion and Infanticide," in *Philosophy and Public Affairs* 2 (Fall 1972): 63.

11. Ibid., 37.

12. Ibid., 65.

13. Rudolph Ehrensing, "When Is It Really Abortion?," *The National Catholic Reporter* (25 May 1966), 4. Martin Buss, writing in 1967, also believed that the onset of brain waves was the logical dividing point for personhood. But in 1967, Buss understood that brain waves appear in a fetus during the seventh month; thus he was led to locate the beginning of human life fairly late in pregnancy, perhaps even at birth itself. One wonders what he might say in light of the fact that brain waves are now detected as early as forty-three days after conception. See Martin Buss, "The Beginning of Human Life as an Ethical Problem," *Journal of Religion* 47 (July 1967): 250.

14. Roy Schenk, "Let's Think About Abortion," *The Catholic World*, April 1968, 16.

15. Joseph Fletcher, "Indicators of Humanhood: A Tentative Profile of Man," *The Hastings Center Report* 2 (November 1972): 1.

16. Peter Singer, "Sanctity of Life or Quality of Life," *Pediatrics* 72 (July 1983): 129.

17. Winston L. Duke, "The New Biology," *Reason*, August 1972.

18. Mary Anne Warren, "On the Moral and Legal Status of Abortion," *The Monist*, January 1973, 55f.

19. Thomas L. Hayes, "A Biological View," *Commonweal*, 17 March 1967, 678.

20. Norman C. Gillespie, "Abortion and Human Rights," *Ethics* 87 (1976): 238.

21. Lederberg, "Geneticist Looks at Contraception," 25-27.

22. Garrett Hardin, "Semantic Aspects of Abortion," *ETC* 24 (September 1967): 278. Note also Hardin's article, "Abortion—Or Compulsory Pregnancy?" *Journal of Marriage and the Family* 30 (May 1968): 246-51.

23. Charles Hartshorne, "Concerning Abortion: An Attempt at a Rational View," *The Christian Century*, 21 January 1981, 42-45.

24. Joseph Fletcher, *Situation Ethics: The New Morality* (Philadelphia: Westminster Press, 1966).

25. Fletcher, *Genetic Control*, 137.

26. Ibid., 143.

27. Ibid.

28. Ibid., 171.

29. Ibid., 138.

30. Joseph Fletcher, "Indicators of Humanhood," 1-4. Fletcher's fifteen positive criteria included: minimal intelligence, self-awareness, self-control, a sense of time, a sense of futurity (purposiveness), a sense of the past (memory), the capability to relate to others, concern for others, ability to communicate, control of one's existence, curiosity, the capacity to change, a balance of rationality and feeling, idiosyncrasy, and neocortical function (the "cardinal indicator"). Fletcher's five negative criteria included: man is not non- or anti-artificial, man is not essentially parental, man is not essentially sexual, man is not a bundle of rights, and man is not a worshiper. I refer you to Fletcher's article for a clearer understanding of this criteria. Space does not permit me to elaborate here.

31. Joseph Fletcher, "Four Indicators of Humanhood—The Enquiry Matures," *The Hastings Center Report* 4 (December 1974): 4-7.

32. Fletcher, *Genetic Control*, 171.

33. Ibid., 135ff.

34. Ibid., 171.

35. Ibid. Fletcher speaks of trying to "keep a straight face" when people argue for fertilization or implantation or the time of quickening as the moment when the fetus becomes a person (p. 139). Yet here, in a much more arbitrary manner, Fletcher chooses criteria which would theoretically allow for an ape to be classified as a human being.

36. Williams, "Medical Abortion," 21.

37. J. Z. Young, *An Introduction to the Study of Man* (London: OUP, 1971), 367f.

38. Jerome Lejeune, in a testimony prepared for the Subcommittee on Separation of Powers of the United States Senate Committee on the Judiciary, and printed in a booklet entitled "The Beginning of Human Life," *Studies in Law and Medicine* (Chicago: Americans United for Life, Inc., 1981), 2. This booklet includes the testimonies of three other distinguished physicians affirming that human life begins at conception. They are Micheline M.

Mathews-Roth, M.D., Hymie Gordon, M.D., F.R.C.P., and Herbert Ratner, M.D.

39. The idea that we are always in a process of development is a fascinating one. For instance, if there is never a point in time when the process is complete, then it follows that you never really have a person. I suppose that all proabortion advocates view themselves as persons. They believe they became persons through a process. Therefore, there had to be a point at which time they became persons, or they have always been persons. Either that, or they are not yet persons!

40. Norman Anderson, *Issues of Life and Death* (Downers Grove, Ill.: InterVarsity Press, 1978), 77f. Actually, Anderson is quoting favorably a sentence from G. Dunstan, *The Artifice of Ethics* (London: SCM Press, 1974), 65.

41. Hayes, "Biological View," 678.

42. In this way, there is no moral conflict in their system. They show respect for life by speaking of the "sanctity of *personal* life." But it is all with an ulterior motive. By redefining prenatal life as potential, they rescind its full value and natural right to live.

43. See my earlier discussion in this chapter about Hardin's and Fletcher's logic of potential versus actual.

44. John Wilke, in *National Right To Life News*, 29 June 1981, 5.

45. Fletcher, *Genetic Control*, 143.

46. Robert E. Joyce, "When Does a Person Begin?" *New Perspectives on Human Abortion*, ed. T. W. Hilgers, D. J. Horan, and D. Mall (Frederick, Maryland: Aletheia Books, 1981), 353.

47. Warren, "Moral and Legal Status," 59.

48. Cf. Gary M. Atkinson, "The Morality of Abortion," *International Philosophical Quarterly* 14 (1974): 350. Roslyn Weiss of Columbia University is right when she argues that the term *potential* is not introduced to help us define the essence of humanity; it has been introduced for the sole purpose of taking away the rights of the unborn. Proabortion apologists want us to consider the fetus as potential life because they do not want the unborn to have rights equal to the mother's. Weiss makes the interesting observation: "Human beings protect themselves with a thicket of rights they do not grant to other beings, and some of these rights are said to be *human* rights—rights one has simply by virtue of being human." Any conceptual uncertainty about the fetus being human would then serve to call in question his rights. See Roslyn Weiss, "The Perils of Personhood," *Ethics* (October 1978), 67.

49. Anderson, *Issues*, 77.

50. R. C. Sproul, *Ethics and the Christian* (Wheaton: Tyndale House, 1983), 82. Sproul is very much against abortion. His line of argument is to take the term *potential* and use it effectively against proabortion arguments by showing the sacredness of potential life. Nevertheless, it would be better to argue that the term *potential* should not be used in the abortion context.

51. Dr. Leon Rosenberg, as reported in *Science*, 22 May 1981, 907.

52. Dr. Alfred M. Bongioanni, as reported in the *National Right to Life News*, 15 June 1981.

53. For our discussion of the unity of body and soul in Scripture, see chapter 4 and the section, "Is Biological Life Essential to Personhood?"

54. Daniel Callahan, *Abortion: Law, Choice, and Morality* (New York: Macmillan, 1970), 393-94. He writes: "If it is possible to define 'human' any way we wish in the instance of prenatal life (according to our reading of social consequences), is there any logical reason why we should not be able to do the same thing with postnatal life? . . . Society (or a power group in society) could, by use of this principle, define the chronically ill, the senile, the elderly as non-human and thus justify the taking of their life on grounds of social good to be obtained" (p. 393). Yet, this same scholar falls into the same illogical trap when he concludes that he prefers to distinguish between species/life, body/life, and person/life. These refer respectively for him to the life of the whole group of *Homo sapiens*, the physical life of individual human beings, and the life of those who may be called persons. This is what you might call "sitting on the fence" (p. 386).

55. This is the situation as of 1 January 1986. The following two years will no doubt see almost all of the states enacting living will legislation.

56. See chapter 4 and the section, "Can Anyone Be Excluded from Personhood?"

57. Sir William Liley, "The Foetus As a Personality," *Creation Research Society Quarterly* 13 (September 1976): 99; reprinted by permission from the *Australian and New Zealand Journal of Psychiatry* 6 (1972).

58. Ibid.

59. Joyce, "When Does a Person Begin?" 355.

60. Fletcher, *Genetic Control*, 142.

61. Notice that the quality of life view is not being used to enhance the quality of life of the handicapped or the young poor. Instead of assuring handicapped newborn of immediate medical attention, it opens wide the door to infanticide. Any infant perceived to be a burden to society due to the cost of helping poor women provide for their newborn can be eliminated. Even if an infant is perfectly healthy and born to a wealthy family, the quality of life euphemism still applies since the unborn is not in the full sense a person; all the mother has to do is not want the child. Curtis Young, executive director of the Christian Action Council in Washington, D.C., is surely on target when he writes that the "quality of life" euphemism "is essentially self-serving, cloaked in the terminology of personal fulfillment, human potential, and self-realization." (Curt Young, *The Least of These* [Chicago: Moody Press, 1983], 24.)

Rather than setting up criteria that deny personhood to the weak, the unborn, and the deformed, we must move toward creating a society in which the lives of all people are valued. Instead of destroying life, we must destroy the conditions that make life intolerable. When children are hungry, neglected, battered, or handicapped, or their capabilities are limited, we must respond in love and service to enhance the dignity of their lives.

62. Archibald Cox, *The Role of the Supreme Court in American Government* (New York: Oxford Press, 1976), 52.

63. Bernard Ramm, "An Ethical Evaluation of Biogenetic Engineering," *Journal of the American Scientific Affiliation* 26 (December 1974): 142.

64. Ronald J. Greer, "Ethical Dimensions of Infanticide" (Paper presented to the Convention of the Southeastern Region, American Association on Mental Deficiency, Religion Division, Jackson, 12 November 1981), 4.

Chapter 3

The Evangelical Response

*H*ow did the evangelical community respond to the abortion thrust of the sixties and seventies? In particular, how did these Bible-believers respond to the redefinition of personhood, so crucial to the debate? Unfortunately, the response has been one of ambivalence and uncertainty. It is true that evangelicals have always been against abortion in general, especially abortion-on-demand. But a closer look at statements by some leading evangelicals reveals major disagreements. Some arguments even appear to align themselves with prochoice logic. For clarity's sake, we will first note the response prior to the 1973 Supreme Court decision.

A Symposium

Of special significance was a symposium held in August 1968, a significant time in the active promotion of abortion. The symposium was sponsored by two leading evangelical organizations, *Christianity Today* and the Christian Medical Society. They met with these goals:

> To study the medical, theological, and legal principles bearing on the problems of contraception,

sterilization and induced abortion with a multidisci-
plinary approach. To seek to establish moral
guidelines for decisions which will be medically
sound, rooted in a biblical ethic and which will be of
pragmatic value to the practicing physician and
minister.[1]

The results of the symposium were presented in the book,
Birth Control and the Christian. Also, a nine-page document,
"A Protestant Affirmation on the Control of Human Reproduction," emerged as the stated consensus of the twenty-five participating scholars.[2]

Because the scholars were evangelical in perspective,
which means (as I understand it) they held to the authority of
Scripture, one would have hoped they could have arrived at a
unified view of what Scripture teaches on this matter.

Instead, the conference was characterized by uncertainty
and a wide range of views. John Warwick Montgomery, among
others, provided strong arguments for the sanctity of unborn
life. He was well aware of the secular distinctions being made
between biological life and personhood, and addressed the
specific criteria being proposed by prochoice logic. Others,
however, were uncertain. Some even came with the clear intent
of supporting abortion.

The final statement of affirmation ended up supporting the
main contentions of the prochoice thrust at that time. The scholars could not agree on a definition of personhood, but they did
agree on liberalizing abortion laws.

The Papers

In the printed papers of the symposium, one scholar after
another appeared to support the view that personhood does not
begin at conception. An Old Testament scholar used Exodus
21:22 as definitive biblical proof that a fetus was not a person
with value equal to the mother: "And if men struggle with each
other and strike a woman with child so that she has a miscarriage, yet there is no further injury, he shall surely be fined as

the woman's husband may demand of him; and he shall pay as the judges decide." This scholar reasoned, since the destruction of the fetus was not a capital offense, apparently God does not regard the fetus as a soul or human being. Therefore, although the fetus has great value, its value is not equal to that of the mother.[3]

A New Testament scholar concluded there is no certainty about the status of the fetus, and therefore abortion is legitimate, though restraint should be taken. He admitted: "I stand as one perplexed, who at one time spoke out in public for a liberal abortion policy because it seemed to me that there was no *final* verdict possible. It still seems that way to me."[4]

A theologian defined the human fetus as "living tissue with a unique genetic makeup, destined to become a fully developed human organism." As to whether or not a fetus has a soul or is made in the divine image, he felt there was no certainty. The least he might say was that the fetus is a "potential person, and maybe it is a primordial person, that is, a person in its most elementary form."[5]

A sociologist, finding no conclusive evidence that a fetus is human, concluded that abortion should not be denied "in cases of rape, incest or disease that might lead to physical and/or mental deformity." He argued that the Christian should not impose his ethics on society. Abortion, he said, is a matter of Christian liberty. He then proposed three factors for Christian families to weigh when considering abortion:

1. What will be the effect on the husband-wife relationship? Will the extra child, "if unwanted," be detrimental to their relationship?

2. What about the personal health of the individuals involved—the father, the mother, and even the child? This is especially important for unmarried mothers.

3. What will be the effect on children already in the family? A Christian couple should arrive at the abortion decision "democratically" with each other.[6]

In a nine-page article, a professor of psychology devoted the first six pages to finding a consensus in secular literature of indications for therapeutic abortion. Then in one sentence he says: "In the absence of specific scriptural or theological guidelines" in this regard, the Christian has one of two options: either consider all abortions "unjustifiable murder," or consider the "evidence" and determine what would be "the mind of Christ" in this matter.[7] He takes the latter approach. This evangelical psychologist made no attempt to deal with biblical principles or even with the deeper psychological problems that could surface following abortions.[8]

Perhaps the most significant article was written by an acknowledged scholar and leader within the evangelical movement. He wrote that a fetus is "potential human life in process of becoming a human being." In a long, carefully thought-out sentence, this scholar offered what he called an alternative hypothesis:

> The human being originates at conception by a traducian process and constitutes a unitary being which is from the first potentially human and thus of immeasurable value, develops a distinguishable but intricately united and interdependent body and spirit, and eventually consummates, as a result of his relationship to God by means of the divine creative will, in a human being who is a divinely-purposed-and-sustained, immortal soul with a body (i.e., body-form).[9]

On the one hand, he says "the human being originates at conception." On the other hand, the fetus is "potentially human . . . and eventually consummates . . . in a human being." He holds to a traducian view of the soul,[10] and yet also says that the fetus's humanity depends on the "divine creative will," which apparently comes at some stage after conception.

His conclusion is that abortion is not manslaughter, since the fetus is not yet man. But abortion is still wrong, since the fetus is "potentially human," and since human life is sacred.[11]

All these statements are significant for two very important reasons. First, these scholars swayed a number of participants toward a more reformist position regarding abortion. (The position was not moderate in the context of the time, but reformist.) For example, one participant, a prominent psychiatrist and physician, remarked that he was convinced of two things when he arrived at the symposium: (1) in the sanctity of human life, and (2) that a new life is created at the moment of conception. But due to the conference, he altered his views. Now he holds that while the fetus may have value in utero, it may be a developing value in concert with the growth of the fetus. And while conception is still the logical point of origin of new life, "perhaps 'human life' as such need not come into existence at a single moment in time." Thus, "the fetus has great and developing value, but is less than a human being." His conclusion was that abortion is permissible in certain cases.[12]

The second reason the scholars' statements were significant was that they provided support for the change in the definition of personhood by the secular world. Instead of challenging the secular view of man, they endorsed the very logic we reviewed in the previous chapter.

The Affirmation Statement

The statement of affirmation that emerged as the consensus of the participating scholars was ambivalent on the definition of personhood: "At the most, [the human fetus] is an actual human life or at the least, a potential and developing human life. . . . From the moment of *birth*, the infant is a human being" (italics mine).[13] It served to confirm the views of the prochoicers.

Also, in regard to legal matters, the statement aligned itself fundamentally with the prochoice forces:

> Changes in the state laws on therapeutic abortion . . . should be encouraged.
>
> Suitable cases for abortion would fall within the scope of the American College of Obstetricians and

Gynecologists Statement on Therapeutic Abortion.

As to whether or not the performance of an induced abortion is always sinful we are not agreed, but about the necessity and permissibility for it under certain circumstances we are in accord.

The Christian physician will advise induced abortion only to safeguard greater values sanctioned by Scripture. These values should include *individual health*, *family welfare*, and *social responsibility* [italics mine].

Much human suffering can be alleviated by preventing the birth of children where there is a predictable high risk of genetic disease or abnormality. This appears to be *a reasonable Christian objective* [italics mine].[14]

These statements are in accord with the statements of the American Law Institute, the American Medical Association, and the American College of Obstetricians and Gynecologists referred to in chapter 1. The symposium ended up supporting the main thrust of the prochoice movement.

Hindsight is better than foresight. Some of these same evangelical scholars have changed their positions since the symposium. But the conference set the pattern for the evangelical response to abortion.

A Minisymposium

In 1971, another major evangelical periodical addressed the abortion issue. *Eternity* magazine solicited the opinions of a number of evangelical scholars whose fields ranged from medicine to theology.[15]

The same breadth of opinion prevailed at the *Eternity* minisymposium as had at the *Christianity Today* symposium. Most of the scholars were at a loss to answer the question of personhood. For some, it centered around when a fetus becomes a living soul. Most were happy to call the fetus a "potential" person.

All participants agreed on the intrinsic value of fetal life, and all denounced the extreme notion that a fetus in its early life is simply a mass of tissue. But most agreed that we should allow for the liberalizing of traditional laws in hard cases.

Those more closely related to the field of medicine were more open to abortion for reasons other than the life of the mother. One went so far as to say that induced abortion should be allowed to safeguard "greater values sanctioned by Scripture." For him, these greater values included family welfare and social responsibilities. Another supposed that with a deformed child on its way, one would have to weigh such factors as the wishes of the parents, their ability to care for the deformed child, and even possibly some wider socioeconomic factors such as population control.[16] As to whether babies with abnormalities should be aborted, at least half appeared open to the idea.

The Rhetoric

We should note a kind of rhetoric that surrounded the articles for limited abortion. Several ideas kept recurring in both symposiums.

First, in an *imperfect world*, sometimes one has to choose between the *lesser of two evils*. The alternative of abortion may be the better solution, while we must constantly be aware of God's love and forgiveness.

Second, we are dealing with *very complex* medical issues, and we cannot come up with *simplistic* rule-of-thumb solutions. While everyone rejected approaches such as situation ethics, they also rejected what they would call an *absolutist* position. Most were uncertain as to what constitutes a legitimate therapeutic reason for abortion. Many found various social, psychological, and personal reasons ethically confusing, but few were willing to deny their validity.

Third, we must *seek God's will* in this matter and *pray* for his direction. Since Scripture does not speak definitively on this issue, we have nothing to pin our decisions on. All we have are biblical principles such as the character of Jesus found in the gospels, the concept of love, and the dignity of human life. But these principles become elusive when applied to abortion.

Today there has developed within the prolife movement the feeling that these spiritual ideas tagged onto arguments for limited abortion are really a form of prochoice rhetoric. This is a legitimate complaint. Invariably in both symposiums, when an evangelical scholar appeared to support opening the door to limited abortion, he did so utilizing these ideas.

POST-*ROE* V. *WADE*

Then a turnaround occurred. Though evangelical leaders had not at first spoken out against abortion, the liberalization of abortion laws—together with the 22 January 1973 Supreme Court decision—made a marked impact on the evangelical community. Scholars began to rethink their positions on abortion as prochoice and prolife literature began to pour forth.

Christianity Today was one of the first to perceive the Supreme Court's anti-Christian bias in its decision to legalize abortion. In a February 1973 issue, an editorial noted that Justice Blackmun had gone to Greek and Roman law and had stated that "ancient religion did not bar abortion." By stating this, Blackmun's opinion clearly referred to paganism, for Judaism and Christianity *did* bar abortion, as we noted in the first chapter.[17]

Books came swiftly off the press in response to the Court's edict. Evangelical scholars such as Harold O. J. Brown, John Warwick Montgomery, Clifford Bosgra, and Richard Ganz began laying the deeper scriptural and social reasons for opposing abortion. Other scholars such as Paul Ramsay, Albert Outler, and J. Robert Nelson contributed to the discussion, even though their own denomination, the United Methodist Church, in 1976 passed a position statement strongly supporting permissive abortion.

Then two special events took place. First, in 1975, evangelical leaders from around the nation met in Billy Graham's home for two days to determine a proper biblical response to abortion-on-demand. Their deliberations resulted in the formation of the Christian Action Council (CAC), which since that time has sought to be both a prophetic and a gospel ministry.[18] The CAC has challenged the existing abortion policy, contributed to the education of the evangelical community, and established alternatives for women with problem pregnancies.

The second event was the production of the film series, *Whatever Happened To The Human Race?*, by Francis Schaeffer and C. Everett Koop.[19] This five-episode series effectively told the story of the growth of abortion, infanticide, and euthanasia in the United States, and showed the methodical erosion of the Judeo-Christian ethos along with the parallel devaluation of man. The series called upon Christians to become involved in a moral reversal of society and provided strategies for doing so.

Seminars were held throughout the United States led by Francis Schaeffer and C. Everett Koop, but attendance was disappointingly low. Many wondered whether Christians really wanted to hear or know so much about abortion. Schaeffer himself suggested the church had already become too closely wed with secular culture and was too comfortable in that marriage to take an aggressive stand against abortion.

Many evangelicals simply did not know the issue; most would not get involved in controversial subjects, and abortion is controversial. It was common to hear Christians say: "I don't get involved in politics"; "We shouldn't impose our morality on others"; "The church should be involved in 'spiritual' matters"; "I believe in the separation of church and state."

For these reasons, the Schaeffers and their associates found it difficult to arouse evangelicals to action. In retrospect, I believe they succeeded. Their film series was a turning point in evangelical involvement.

Perhaps the change in mood of the evangelicals from 1973 to the present is best typified by the change that took place in Dr. Koop's own views. In his book, *The Right To Live: The Right To Die*, Koop tells how he originally believed there was room for abortion in hard cases. But when states began liberalizing their abortion laws, Koop had a change of mind. Apparently the testimony of a registered nurse spoken at the right time, together with further reflection on Scripture, convinced him of the right to life of all the unborn.[20]

Professor Bruce K. Waltke, the Old Testament scholar in the 1967 symposium who argued from Exodus 21:22 that a fetus is not a person with value equal to the mother, made an about-face. Delivering his presidential address at the twenty-seventh annual meeting of the Evangelical Theological Society in 1975, Waltke admitted that his former position was "less than conclusive for both exegetical and logical reasons," and his conclusion now was that the fetus is indeed a human being and that abortion is murder.[21]

Another example of a change of mind is Jean Garton, who was involved for a time in working to legalize abortion. Then, in the process of intensive study and reflection on Scripture, medicine, and law, she says (quoting C. S. Lewis), "I was carried kicking and screaming" into the prolife position "by the sheer weight of the evidence." Jean Garton has written one of the most effective books exposing prochoice slogans, *Who Broke The Baby?*[22]

Jim Wallis, editor of *Sojourners* magazine, also had a change of heart on this issue. *Sojourners* is an evangelical monthly magazine committed to fighting racism, poverty, and violence in all its forms. In an editorial in a 1980 issue devoted to the abortion question, Wallis notes that it was "only a matter of time before the spiritual logic of these other commitments would lead us to a 'pro-life' response to abortion as well."[23]

Sojourners' active support for the unborn shows the breadth of the prolife movement. Many Christians tend to think of "Moral Majority types" when looking at prolifers. But

Sojourners' special issue on abortion included essays by antiwar activists, feminists, and civil rights proponents. They were all speaking out on behalf of the unborn.

THE CONSENSUS GROWS

By 1980, fifty-nine of ninety-nine denominations had either adopted formal resolutions opposing abortion or had indicated in other ways their strong opposition. Another fifteen denominations had gone on record as opposed to abortion in general, but willing to allow for one or more of the hard cases. Eleven denominations refused to take any stand whatsoever; the remaining fourteen expressed support for abortion-on-demand.[24] (Of course, the Roman Catholic Church throughout the entire two decades remained firm in its opposition to abortion.)

In 1980, the evangelical family magazine *Moody Monthly* devoted an entire issue to abortion. The editor challenged the readers to explain why evangelicals were not yet fully involved in the issue. His editorial bemoaned, "Evangelicalism as a whole has uttered no real outcry. We've organized no protest. Do we need more time to think abortion through? Isn't seven years long enough? . . . The Catholics have called abortion, 'The Silent Holocaust.' The deeper horror is the silence of the evangelical."[25]

Of course, 1980 was an election year, and the phenomenon of "The New Right" became prominent. Some within this movement had an agenda that ran counter to some of the thinking within the prolife movement as a whole. A polarization began to develop, a polarization whose impact is still too early to fully assess.

But this much is certain. The prolife movement includes supporters from both ends of the political spectrum, even among evangelicals. In spite of such differences, the prolife movement within the evangelical community has been moving toward a consensus on abortion. More and more evangelicals are overwhelmingly against abortion, and more are doubting the validity of the hard cases, especially of therapeutic abortion.

Another Good Example

One of the clearest and most complete reversals of position has been that of Norman L. Geisler, presently professor of systematic theology at Dallas Theological Seminary. In the early seventies, Geisler argued in his widely used textbook, *Ethics: Alternatives and Issues*, that the unborn are only potential persons and that abortion is justified in certain medical or social circumstances.[26] The book was a classic example of the reasoning behind the views of many evangelicals who view themselves as prolife and yet justify abortion in certain hard cases.

Geisler argued that abortion is not necessarily murder "because the embryo is not fully human—it is an undeveloped person."[27] Personhood should be equated with self-awareness and the ability to relate to others:

> The determining factor as to whether or not one is a 'person' is whether or not they can function with some measure of self-consciousness and freedom. If they are subjects who can love and understand that they are being loved, then they are persons and ought to be kept alive as such at all cost.[28]

Geisler asked, When might abortion be justified? First, in a clear-cut case when the life of the mother is at stake. For the actual life of the mother "is of more intrinsic value" than the potential life of the unborn.[29]

Is it ever right to take the life of a fetus when we know it will be deformed, retarded, or subhuman? If a life can be shown to be subhuman, he had argued, this would constitute a "higher moral reason for nipping a life before it buds." (This might be the case with mongolism.)[30]

What about rape and incest? Abortion may be justified in such cases, for conception occurred without the mother's consent. "A violent intrusion into a woman's womb does not bring with it a moral birthright for the embryo." The violation of her honor was bad enough, Geisler felt, without compelling her to carry an unwanted baby to term.[31]

Now, however, Geisler has changed his position. In an article written to deal with the hard cases and other prochoice arguments, Geisler begins by arguing that "the Bible leaves no doubt that the God who makes man in His image and likeness (Genesis 1:27) does this in the womb before birth." At no time from conception on is the unborn anything but "a tiny, growing human being," and self-consciousness is not a test for humanness.[32]

Clearly, then, while rape or incest is an awful experience, the child conceived is still an innocent life, and two wrongs do not make a right. Moreover, while there may be some deformed or retarded babies, they are still human, and "everyone has a right to the life he actually has."[33]

What caused Geisler to change his position so completely? The key was the change in his view of the unborn as human beings from conception. Geisler is now actively involved in prolife activities. He is a good example of many evangelicals who, after considering the issue of abortion in depth, choose life. Changes of view such as this show that a consensus is growing.

DISSENTING VOICES

While we find the Koops and Waltkes and Geislers and *Sojourners* crossing over the rift in the abortion debate, the rift remains. We evangelicals still lack a consensus. In fact, there are notable scholars who, though clearly against abortion-on-demand, still hold to arguments that are in line with prochoice logic. Here are several prominent examples.

An Ethicist

Lewis B. Smedes is professor of theology and ethics at Fuller Theological Seminary. An able scholar, he has attempted to provide tools for handling the moral ambiguities we meet in life. In his exposition of the sixth commandment, Smedes defines a person this way:

The concrete person, beautiful or ugly, productive or idle, smart or stupid, is the one whom God made, whom God loves, whose life is in God's hands, and for whom his Son died on the cross. This is the person who walks humbly on earth as the image and likeness of the Creator who made him. We do not have to agree about what particular feature marks him as God's image—intellect, creativity, or maybe sexuality. In any case, he is, with all his gifts and in spite of all his sins, the sacred person among all other valuable living creatures.[34]

This definition would fit in nicely with a prolife stance. Does not Scripture present the unborn child as someone "whom God made, whom God loves, and whose life is in God's hands"? Nor does Smedes appear to be caught up in defining what qualities or accomplishments are necessary for personhood.

Yet he makes this critical distinction: He prefers to speak of the "sacredness of persons" rather than the "sanctity of life." He wants to be known as being "pro-person" rather than "pro-life."[35] Then he says, we have to face the question as to whether a "sacred person is actually present in the life that is in my hands."[36] How do we recognize a person when we see him or her?

For him, this question erodes any firm basis for addressing the morality of abortion. We know, says Smedes, that abortion is the killing of human life. But is that human life a person? Some believe a fetus is a person from conception. But this "exposes a deep ontological ambiguity—the ambiguity of not being something yet and at the same time having the makings of what it will be." The fact that a fetus is "*only* potential" life means that it is not yet a person. "An acorn is not an oak tree, even if it has sprouts; and no one in his right mind would equate crushing an acorn with cutting down an oak tree."[37] (Joseph Fletcher, you may recall, used this same analogy.)

Smedes adds that some suppose that a fetus becomes a person at some particular moment, such as quickening, or viability, or the presence of brain waves. But are such indicators enough to show fetal personhood? Others say a fetus becomes a person when it is born. But the only thing that changes at birth is that the baby now breathes air on its own power.[38]

Smedes concludes that the fetus develops into personhood gradually:

> We are inclined to think of becoming a person as a process. But the hypothesis that the fetus gradually develops into the fulness of what a person is deprives us of clear-cut positions and certain absolutes. We eliminate the absolute anti-abortionism of people who believe a fetus is a person the instant an egg is fertilized. We eliminate the absolutism of pro-abortionists who believe that a fetus becomes a person only after it is born. The premise that fetal life is person-becoming life imposes on us the moral burden of protecting fetal life; we will be anti-abortion as a state of mind.[39]

At this point, Smedes brings up several "What if . . ." arguments. What if a child is conceived by a woman who is raped, or who has been seduced by an incestuous father, or who has many children and the father is a heavy drinker? What if a woman gets pregnant in an act of adultery and her husband will have nothing to do with her carrying the child? What if the child has Tay-Sachs disease and is already condemned to die by the age of two? Do not these needs rule out an absolutist position against abortion?

He concludes, no one can ever know for sure that in a particular case abortion is justified—but it would need to be done during the first six weeks of pregnancy. Then comes the rhetoric which so often accompanies such a view:

> Every person who, on balancing out the claims of the fetus and the needs of others, decides for abortion, will need to do it with fear and trembling before God and conscience, taking the risk that she may be doing

something deeply wrong, and trusting a forgiving God to carry her through.[40]

Smedes finds himself then in a real dilemma. On the one hand, he cannot accept that a fetus is a person from conception. On the other hand, he does not want to admit that the fetus at the later stages of pregnancy is a nonperson. He asks, Is there a workable legal response possible, since neither prolife or proabortion absolutist positions are acceptable? The present abortion-on-demand is morally intolerable. But the opposite option could carry society to cruel consequences of its own. What is his answer?

(1) Abortion should be legally permitted during the first six weeks of pregnancy since no one can reasonably be sure that the fetus is a person at that time.

(2) Abortion should be severely restricted after the first six weeks and through the twelfth week, since serious defects cannot be found until the twelfth week.

(3) Abortion after the third month should be a crime, since by that time a fetus has obviously developed into a functioning human body like a person.[41]

In response, even if we were to concede that the unborn are not yet persons during the first six weeks of pregnancy and still wanted to guard against abortion-on-demand, Smede's guidelines are unrealistic. Virtually all abortions are performed after six weeks simply because it takes that long for women to realize they are pregnant and make a decision for abortion. By leaving the door open for abortion through the twelfth week so that serious defects can be found, is Smedes suggesting that all babies be tested? Besides, this is an open door for abortion-on-demand.

Smedes advocates that a woman should, with fear and trembling, do what she thinks at least might be wrong. But "he who doubts is condemned . . . and whatever is not from faith is sin" (Romans 14:23). If abortion is permitted because God is a forgiving God who can carry you through, why not "continue in sin that grace might increase?" (Romans 6:1). As Paul has already said, "May it never be!"

A Founding Father

Carl F. H. Henry is the author of approximately thirty books and editor of a dozen more. When Henry speaks, evangelicals listen—especially when he speaks on social concerns. Many credit Henry's 1947 book, *An Uneasy Conscience of Fundamentalism*, as primarily responsible for the fresh awareness of the social dimension of the gospel among evangelicals.[42]

In a recent essay, Henry sought to stimulate study and discussion by presenting some of his personal views on public policies. Henry holds, for example, that the purpose of civil government is to preserve justice and promote peace and order in fallen society. Moral absolutes do exist, due to the sovereignty of a righteous God. Christians are then obligated to promote justice and to protest injustice wherever it exists. Henry's concern for the poor, the sanctity of the family, and the active pursuit of peace in the world are welcomed by all who are prolife.

When he tackles the abortion issue, Henry finds abortion-on-demand to be evil, the "most horrendous injustice" of this generation. He says, "the ready sacrifice of fetal life as a means of sexual gratification and of birth control is monstrous."

But he also says:

> When childbirth would endanger the mother's life abortion can be morally justifiable. The fetus seems less than human, moreover, in cases of extreme deformity in which rational and moral capacities integral to the *imago Dei* are clearly lacking. The scriptural correlation of sexual intercourse with marriage and the family, furthermore, implies an ethical basis for voluntary abortion in cases of incest and rape.[43]

This statement, when examined carefully, leaves much to be desired for someone who professes to be for the unborn. First, the question of endangering the mother's life is moot. It never should have been an important issue in the modern debate since medicine has made this possibility such a rare circumstance, and since laws have always allowed for the life of the mother to be spared.

Henry's statement also leaves open the possibility of aborting severely handicapped children. Indeed, it assumes that one would have to determine through amniocentesis or some other method whether the unborn child was so handicapped. How is it possible to determine early in pregnancy to what extent a child is handicapped? Is Henry saying that a child must measure up to certain "rational and moral" standards to assume the *imago Dei*? Surely the unborn child's worth is not to be based on what "seems" to be less than human from our limited perspective.

Rape and incest certainly are horrible experiences. But how can the fact that intercourse took place outside of the marriage relationship be used as the moral basis for justifying abortion in these cases? Are we to believe that only those conceived in a marriage relationship are sacred? Are all those conceived outside of marriage open to abortion? We should note that the majority of abortions are done for women conceiving out of wedlock.

These are difficult issues Henry addresses, to be sure, and we will address them further in chapter 6. But those of us in the prolife movement are very aware that these were the issues that historically opened the door to abortion-on-demand, the very thing Henry abhors. His ambivalence about the worth of the unborn can lead to the "horrendous injustice" he wishes to end. It is not without reason that there are no prolife groups in Washington arguing for exceptions in the hard cases, for in reality this would guarantee the continuance of abortion-on-demand.

An Institution

At Wheaton College in the fall of 1984, strong feelings surfaced when the student government invited interested students to a meeting to discuss adopting a resolution against abortion. The proposed resolution read:

Whereas, Since the Roe v. Wade Supreme Court decision of 1973 over 15 million unborn children have lost their lives in legalized abortions in the United States,

Whereas, The practice of infanticide is growing and has received limited legal sanction,

Whereas, Euthanasia has become a likely future prospect for the aged and handicapped,

Whereas, In the medical communities and legal structures of American society a so-called "quality" of life determination has replaced the ethic of the sanctity of human life,

Resolved, The Student Government of Wheaton College affirms that all human life from conception to natural death is sacred before God and must be protected under law.

Resolved, The Student Government of Wheaton College further encourages the administration of Wheaton College to take an unequivocal, public stand for the sanctity of human life in its long standing tradition of social concern.[44]

The students who penned the statement were hardly prepared for the criticism that followed. At the meeting, heated debate occurred among the collegians attending. Not only was there no agreement to take an immediate stand, but a revised resolution against abortion-on-demand was placed on a back burner. An editorial in the school newspaper opined that the student government was not meant to represent students morally. A letter to the editor argued that a liberal arts education was devoted to "the free play of ideas which are offered for honest, unbiased evaluation," and "only those actions specifically marked as morally evil in the Bible are restricted for members of [the Wheaton College] community."[45]

Then on 25 January 1985, the *Wheaton Record* quoted two professors on their views of abortion. One professor said: "In

biological terms, there is no question that a fetus is human life."
But there is a difference between biological life and persons. It
"takes more than a fertilized ovum to produce a person." A person is self-conscious and reflective, "relating to God and
others." The professor argued that his view was the traditional
evangelical view worked through long ago by scholars (i.e., the
1968 symposium). He was not proabortion, and any abortion
would have to have "overwhelming moral justification" to be acceptable.

The second professor argued that the Bible raised questions that prevented "grounding an anti-abortion position in the
Bible as an absolute, universal law." This professor said he was
antiabortion, but also agreed that a *person* is distinct from a
fetus. A fetus is only a "potential" person, and personhood must
be understood as "a mass of experiences that shape who we
are."[46]

The Wheaton students' position on this issue is, perhaps,
understandable. College is a time to compare, reflect, learn. But
what kinds of instruction were they receiving? Are the two professors not aware of the distinction between biological life and
personhood being made in prochoice circles? I can hardly believe that this is so. Why should we hold on to a supposed "traditional evangelical view" put forth in 1968 when that view was
not the consensus of the church historically and when many of
those who held that view are changing their positions?

"I'M AGAINST ABORTION, BUT . . ."

Such statements are sufficient to show that we evangelicals have not yet arrived at a consensus—and that those who
do not wish to take a firm stand on behalf of all the unborn often
use arguments totally in line with prochoice thought.

What is most troubling is that, in all cases cited, the evangelical spokesmen wanted to be known as standing against abortion. Yet the positions they hold are built upon the same founda-
tions as the positions of those advocating prochoice.

It reminds me of an interview the Wheaton student paper conducted with a woman who worked for the National Abortion Rights Action League in Chicago. Although her whole life is devoted to assuring the continuation of the present abortion policy, she ends the interview by saying, "I'm personally opposed to abortion too."[47]

Brave New People

The most graphic demonstration of the lack of consensus among evangelicals was a book, *Brave New People*, written by D. Gareth Jones and published by InterVarsity Press (IVP) in 1984. Dr. Jones is a professor of anatomy at Otago University in New Zealand. While the book concerns itself with a wide range of bioethical issues, it includes a chapter on "therapeutic abortion."[48]

Action Line, the monthly newsletter of the Christian Action Council, published a review of the book that was strongly critical of Jones's position. IVP's criticisms of the review and CAC's defenses of the review flew back and forth. The result was that the book was finally withdrawn by Inter-Varsity Christian Fellowship (IVCF), parent organizaion of IVP.[49]

Why all the fuss? The book, though written by an evangelical who believes in the authority of God's Word, was perceived by the Christian Action Council and others to be supportive of abortion. In a letter to concerned supporters, the president of IVCF explained that he had no intention of supporting abortion through publishing this book. But since it was being perceived in this way, rather than detract from the campus ministries of the organization, he would prefer to withdraw the book. This was the first time in IVP's forty-three-year history that one of its books had been withdrawn.[50]

Was there any basis for the perception that *Brave New People* supported abortion? Unfortunately there was. Jones's volume is a classic example of an evangelical caught up in the confusion of prochoice rhetoric. Jones uses all the cliches of the prochoice movement (e.g., "each fetus is a human life . . . a potential person . . . well on the road to full personhood"; the fetus is "on its way to becoming an actual person"; achieving personhood is a "continuing process"). He says, "I do not wish to draw a line between when a fetus *is not a person* and when a fetus *is a person.* Nor, says Jones, can biology be used to help determine humanness.[51]

All the clichés and logic of the prochoicers are there. Of course, there is a crucial difference. Jones is not for abortion-on-demand. Fletcher and the other prochoice thinkers we have quoted are. But Jones's position could, taken logically, allow for abortion-on-demand. His criteria for the legitimacy of therapeutic abortion are elastic enough to permit a variety of circumstances.

In a chapter entitled "The Ethics of Therapeutic Abortion," Jones notes that genetic grounds for abortion are gaining in importance. The discovery of various genetic and chromosomal anomalies before birth brings with it the legal option of choice. While abortion is no "cure" for the fetus, says Jones, this matter should be approached within a certain framework:

> In such instances, if abortion is contemplated, a responsible decision will take into account the fetus, and also the parents and siblings. However, any decision to deprive a fetus of its potential for life is a weighty one, depending as it does on the conclusion that the detrimental effects of the birth will outweigh the benefits such a life may bring. At its highest such a decision will take account of the severity of the genetic disorder and the quality of life the afflicted child would probably have had; the physical, emotional and economic impact on the family and society; the reliability of diagnosis; and the increase in the load of detrimental genes in the population if the afflicted individual later has children of his or her own.[52]

In outlining his position in this way, Jones is clearly following the logic of a 1974 World Council of Churches' report that he outlined earlier in his book. Remember that the WCC is admittedly prochoice. Yet their position as stated here by Jones is virtually identical to Jones's:

> According to this outline, abortion should be considered only when any detriment resulting from the birth of the fetus outweighs the potential benefits. The criteria suggested include: i. the severity of the genetic disorder and its effect on the possibility of a meaningful life; ii. the physical, emotional and economic impact on family and society; iii. the availability of adequate medical management and of special educational facilities; iv. the reliability of diagnosis; v. the recognition that an individual genetically defective in one respect may be superior in others; vi. the increase in the load of detrimental genes in the population that may result from the reproduction of carriers of genetic diseases.[53]

Jones then proceeds to consider the status of the fetus. "Fetuses are human beings; they are genetically part of the species, *Homo sapiens*." But fetuses are not yet persons; they are merely "potential persons" developing into "actual persons." Furthermore, Jones says, if the course of development proceeds "normally," then one day the fetus will "attain full personhood in its own right."[54]

Jones argues for what he calls the "potentiality principle." This assumes several points. Not only is the fetus merely a *potential* person, but achieving personhood is a *continuing process*. At the end of that process emerges "an individual human being characterized by full human personhood."[55] When that point is reached is "somewhat nebulous":

> A new-born baby is a very incomplete human person, with an enormous amount of biological development, range of environmental influences and wealth of educational experiences still required for normal maturity and growth. These constitute some of the

relationships so necessary for the developmental continuum to be brought to fruition.[56]

Since the fetus is a potential person, it has "a claim to life and respect." On the other hand, this claim is qualified by the stage of its development. The claim "becomes stronger with development until, at birth, the potential person is so similar to an actual person that the consequences of killing it are practically the same as killing a young person."[57] Jones then concludes:

> In the light of these considerations I believe the potentiality principle is an option for Christians. Its high view of the status of the fetus means that, in practical terms, the fetus will be protected under all normal circumstances. Any circumstances not considered normal will be discussed in a later section.[58]

The key phrase is "under all normal circumstances." We turn then to the later section where he discusses those circumstances not considered normal. They are, Jones emphasizes, "only the most extreme of circumstances." They are "appalling dilemmas," "compromises," which may only be resolved by therapeutic abortion.[59]

What are these circumstances? First are those situations relating to the mental health of the mother. There are family situations where "inadequacy, marital breakdown, financial stringency, unemployment and a host of other adverse social conditions" could lead to the conclusion that abortion would be "the least tragic of a number of tragic options."[60]

Second are those situations involving a severely deformed child. Some families simply cannot cope with such a situation, and therefore "termination of the pregnancy" must be "reluctantly adopted." Of course, this will always be "a last resort." But Christians should always take into account "the mental, spiritual and financial resources of the family and also the availability of social and welfare services for handicapped children in the community."[61]

Jones claims his position differs little from a strong anti-abortion stance.[62] But these circumstances are those presently supported by prochoicers for abortion-on-demand. One can hardly say, as Jones attempts to say, that these are the "most extreme of circumstances."

What is the biblical basis for Jones's position? Jones contends that the Bible does not place an absolute value on human life. If this is true, he says, then the fetus does not have an unqualified right to life.[63]

Moreover, he finds that biblical data relevant to abortion are "scant." The Bible does not speak of the unborn as possessing personhood; nor does it condemn abortion in any passage.[64] Exodus 21:22-25 is not clear. Psalm 139:13-16 and Luke 1:41-44 "should not be made to signify too much." While the Bible places great value on life in the womb, this does not mean that "the fetus is to be equated with a living person." The fetus is merely "being built into the image and likeness of God," and this is all that the Bible means.[65]

The point here is not that Jones's treatment of Scripture was superficial (though, in my opinion, it was). The point is that the book demonstrates a continuing lack of consensus among evangelicals regarding abortion. Not only did InterVarsity Press publish it as an antiabortion book, but a number of leading evangelicals who reviewed it thought it was too!

One of the reviewers, a prolific writer and scholar, called it "an essentially anti-abortion book." A seminary professor said it handled the "biblical data responsibly, and is conservative both in its basic theological stance and in its ethical conclusions." Another reviewer thought that "Jones rarely commits himself to any position that would not be comfortable to the majority of conservative Christians who are well informed, including the best of the pro-life advocates."

Who is fooling whom? Can we not see the similarity between Jones's position and that of the prochoice advocates? Is there no logic? Can Jones use the same terms and rhetoric as the prochoicers and mean something different?

Jones's volume and the controversy it raised show the lack of an evangelical consensus. However, the withdrawal of his book by IVP also shows that evangelicals are more unified today than they were only a few years ago. Jones's book would have been highly acclaimed in 1968 at the evangelical symposium. Even if Jones had written in the seventies, his book would have been well received. For example, Norman Anderson's *Issues of Life and Death*, also printed by IVP in 1978, held similar views and used the same terms—*process, potential,* and *becoming a human being.* Yet there was no uproar.[66]

But Jones's views are now dated, and the time lapse has convinced many evangelicals that Jones's position is an accommodation to the spirit of this age. This was the reason for the uproar over its publication. People are tired of the "middle ground" position. Like dissenters against Vietnam in the sixties, they see the carnage taking place against innocent victims, and they want it stopped.

WHY NOT PROCHOICE?

What is at the root of the ambivalence of some evangelicals toward the abortion issue? The basic premises of Jones, Smedes, and other Christians who have argued for limited abortion are actually quite similar to prochoice logic. Why then do they decline to move fully into the prochoice camp?

Smedes's position that a fetus develops into a person gradually is the same as that of prochoice thinkers. His claim that a number of social problems such as inadequacy and unemployment may take precedence over the unborn's life is no different from the main prochoice arguments of our day. Why then does he want to be known as fundamentally against abortion?

Given the supposed lack of scriptural guidelines, why are most evangelicals still generally against abortion? Is there something inherent in our system of doctrine or thought that subconsciously compels us toward only one side of the issue?

I believe we can discover something that impels Christians toward a prolife position. That discovery concerns the teaching of Scripture. Is Scripture really all that vague about the abortion issue? Can we not challenge prochoice logic from a biblical point of view? Would a more thorough analysis of the themes and texts of Scripture relevant to abortion serve to bring about a consensus among evangelicals? This we intend to find out.

Chapter 3, Notes

1. *Birth Control and the Christian*, ed. Spitzer and Saylor (Wheaton: Tyndale House, 1969), xviii.

2. Ibid., xxiii-xxxi.

3. Ibid., 10-11. This scholar, Dr. Bruce Waltke, has more recently changed his view, as we have noted later in this chapter.

4. Ibid., 44-45.

5. Ibid., 55, 63.

6. Ibid., 324-25.

7. Ibid., 307.

8. Ibid., 301-9.

9. Ibid., 556, 553.

10. The traducian view holds that the soul or spiritual dimension of a person is transmitted seminally from parents to child. Another view, creationism, holds that God creates each soul separately and implants it into the zygote at conception.

11. *Birth Control*, 557.

12. Ibid., 212-13; cf. also p. xix of the introduction which states that the views of some of the participants were significantly changed by the symposium.

13. Ibid., xxv-xxvi.

14. Ibid., xxx, xxviii-xxix, xxv, xxvi, xxx.

15. "Abortion: Can an Evangelical Consensus Be Found?" *Eternity*, February 1971, 16-28.

16. Ibid., 24, 26.

17. *Christianity Today*, 16 February 1973, 32-33. For Blackmun's opinion, see *Roe* v. *Wade*, 410 U.S. 113 (1973), pp. 130-32.

18. Christian Action Council, 701 West Broad Street, Suite 405, Falls Church, VA 22046.

19. In addition to the film series, Schaeffer and Koop also published a book by the same title: Francis A. Schaeffer and C. Everett Koop, *Whatever Happened to the Human Race* (Old Tappan, N.J.: Fleming H. Revell Co., 1979).

20. C. Everett Koop, *The Right to Live: The Right to Die* (Wheaton: Tyndale House Publishers, 1976), 13-15.

21. Bruce K. Waltke, "Reflections from the Old Testament on Abortion," *Journal of the Evangelical Theological Society* 19 (1976) :3.

22. Jean Garton, preface to *Who Broke the Baby?* (Minneapolis: Bethany House Publishers, 1979).

23. *Sojourners*, November 1980, 3.

24. Tj. Bosgra, *Abortion, the Bible, and the Church* (Honolulu: Hawaii Right to Life Educational Foundation, 1980), 31-35.

25. *Moody Monthly*, May 1980, 21.

26. Norman L. Geisler, *Ethics: Alternatives and Issues* (Grand Rapids: Zondervan Publishing House, 1971), 218-27. See also Geisler's book, *The Christian Ethic of Love* (Grand Rapids: Zondervan Publishing House, 1973).

27. Ibid., 219.

28. Ibid., 124.

29. Ibid., 220.

30. Ibid., 221f.

31. Ibid., 222f.

32. Norman L. Geisler, "The Bible, Abortion, and Common Sense," *Fundamentalist Journal*, May 1985, 25.

33. Ibid., 26.

34. Lewis B. Smedes, *Mere Morality* (Grand Rapids: Wm. B. Eerdmans Publishing Co., 1983), 106.

35. Ibid., 105.

36. Ibid., 107.

37. Ibid., 129.

38. Ibid., 129-32.

39. Ibid., 134.

40. Ibid., 135-38.

41. Ibid., 143-44.

42. Carl F. H. Henry, *An Uneasy Conscience of Fundamentalism* (Grand Rapids: Wm. B. Eerdmans Publishing Co., 1947).

43. Carl F. H. Henry, *The Christian Mindset in a Secular Society: Promoting Evangelical Renewal and National Righteousness* (Portland, Ore.: Multnomah Press, 1984), 102-3.

44. "Abortion to Be Resolved," *The Wheaton Record*, 12 October 1984, 2.

45. *The Wheaton Record*, 26 October 1984.

46. *The Wheaton Record*, 25 January 1985. A couple of professors were also quoted who hold to the traditional prolife position.

47. Ibid.

48. D. Gareth Jones, *Brave New People* (Downers Grove, Ill.: Inter-Varsity Press, 1984). Dr. Jones has taught in medical schools in the United States and Australia, received his medical degree from the University of Lon-

don, and is the author of a number of books. Jones also wrote an article in an issue of the *Christian Medical Society Journal* 14 (1 November 1983) :4-7, entitled "Abortion: Some Thoughts on a Perplexing Problem." His arguments in the article parallel those in the book.

49. *Action Line*, the Christian Action Council newsletter, 22 May 1984.

50. The letter was signed by James McLeish and dated 29 August 1984. *Brave New People* by D. Gareth Jones is now being published by Wm. B. Eerdmans Publishing Co.

51. Ibid., 174, 175, 163, 174, 87. The closest Jones comes to providing a precise list of characteristics of humanness or personhood is on p. 80. He qualifies the list by saying that it "is unlikely to prove watertight in all circumstances. However, a start has to be made somewhere. My suggestion is that humanness includes potential or actual awareness of God, a potential capability or actual capability of, for example, conceptual thought, self-awareness, self-consciousness and creativity. Human beings also manifest capacities for love and concern, they relate to others and seek personal fulfillment. All these do not have to be present for humanness to be manifested and yet a potential for most of them is required." Jones continues by arguing: "This follows from our creation in the likeness of a personal God, who has made us living beings capable (or potentially capable) of responding to him and to each other." This list reminds us of Joseph Fletcher's list reviewed in chapter 2. Jones finds it difficult to pin down the main characteristics of humanness; it is always an elusive concept when using the proabortion assumptions of process and potential.

52. Ibid., 157-58.

53. Ibid., 61-62.

54. Ibid., 162-63. Jones makes a separation between human beings and persons. Joseph Fletcher separates human life from human beings/persons. The terminology is different, but the concepts are the same.

55. Ibid., 162-64.

56. Ibid., 175.

57. Ibid., 163. Jones argues in much the same way Garrett Hardin does (see our discussion in chapter 2), when he says: "although the fetus is a member of *Homo sapiens*, a 6-day-old embryo differs in profound respects from a 6-month-old fetus. Once again, this does not justify doing whatever one likes with the 6-day-old embryo; it is *human material* [italics mine] to be treated with care, dignity and respect. Nevertheless, the young embryo is much further from manifesting the qualities of full human personhood than is the 6-month-old fetus, and its chances of doing so are much less than are those of the older fetus."

58. Ibid., 164.

59. Ibid., 176, 181, 177.

60. Ibid., 177.

61. Ibid., 179, 182.

62. Ibid., 173.

63. Ibid., 176. Jones's magazine article is clearer on this issue; see his *Christian Medical Society Journal* article, p. 6.

64. Ibid., 169-70. It is true the Bible does not speak of the unborn as persons. But it is also true the Bible does not ascribe personhood to the born. Personhood as it is being used in the abortion debate and in modern legal contexts is absent from Scripture and alien to its spirit.

65. Ibid., 169-73; the entire biblical discussion takes only four full pages. Early in the book, Jones does discuss in general the image of God and related ideas, pp. 14-28.

66. Norman Anderson, *Issues of Life and Death* (Downers Grove, Ill.: InterVarsity Press, 1976), 75-84.

Chapter 4

What Does Scripture Say about Life and Death?

*M*ost evangelical Christians agree, at least on the surface, that abortion is wrong; few would put themselves entirely in the prochoice camp by approving abortion-on-demand. But evangelicals still disagree about circumstances under which abortion is deemed justifiable or not justifiable.

If the Christian is to believe abortion is wrong, he should do so for sound biblical reasons. Nothing short of careful biblical analysis will do. Why then does such a variety of opinions exist among those who claim the Bible as their life guide? Not all are sure the Bible really speaks to the abortion question. Some believe the Bible is silent on the issue. Others find a few texts indirectly relevant but not clear enough to decide for or against abortion. When seeking to apply the biblical principles they do find relevant, such as those of the sanctity of human life and the need to act in love, they find the answers to the abortion question elusive.

Granted, the Bible is not a textbook on biology. But I do not think the Bible's stand on the abortion issue is as enigmatic as some might suppose. God's Word is still adequate to respond to the bioethical issues of our day, and especially to abortion. My purpose in this chapter is not to produce a litany of proof texts to support my conclusions. Instead I will focus on some main themes of Scripture, and what proof texts there may be will be viewed in light of the total biblical picture.

In chapter 2, we saw the terms and logic of the prochoice point of view, which defines personhood according to arbitrary quality-of-life criteria. We need to examine this definition of personhood from the perspective of Scripture, organizing our reflection around the basic issues prochoice advocates raise.

In this chapter, we want to seek out answers to the following questions concerning human life in general: What is a person? Can anyone be excluded from personhood? Is "biological life" different from personhood? Does Scripture place an absolute value on human life? Is death ever a good alternative in a personal or social dilemma?

In the chapter that follows, we will seek answers to questions that concern unborn life in particular: When does the Bible indicate that human life begins? What level of value does God set on unborn life? Do any passages devalue the unborn? How does Scripture view development in the womb?

WHAT IS A PERSON?

How does the Bible define personhood? This is the core question for Christians facing the abortion issue today. We have noted how the word *person* is a technical term in constitutional law to denote those who have a right to equal protection under law. As abortion clinics across the land continue to take in clients by the thousands, the need to come to some kind of agreement on the definition of person is crucial.

Our first difficulty is that *person* is not used in the Bible. Yes, you can find it in some modern English translations, but there it is derived not from the original text but from the Latin translation of it. Certain Latin versions had used the Latin term *persona* to translate Hebrew and Greek words for man, soul, and face.[1] But it was not an exact equivalent. The difference is quite a significant one.

Persona referred originally to the mask through which an actor spoke his part (*per-sona*; literally, through-mask). From being applied to the mask, it became applied to the actor, then to the character acted, then to an assumed character, then to anyone having character or status.[2] In all these uses, the word *person* describes the individual in terms of his actions and expressions, his roles and functions: the individual as he *performs* in society. This sense is quite limited in comparison to the biblical terms *man* and *soul*.

Because the term *person* historically has accented the *performance* of an individual, it has suited the needs of those who wish to define personhood in terms of discernible functions such as thinking, acting, or feeling. A differentiation can then be made between *person* and the broader term *human*. Then, if "person" characteristics are absent to any degree in a human (such as an unborn child), the right to equal protection under law can be dismissed.

Obviously, the Bible does not have an exact equivalent of the term *person* as used in the abortion controversy. The Bible uses *man* and *woman*, *life* and *soul*—terms much deeper and more significant than *person*. In Scripture, man (generically) is of great worth! This biblical view of man is apparent in chapter 1 of Genesis and unfolds throughout the entire Bible.

Image of God

God's creation of man, as portrayed in Scripture, is singular and striking. Man is not a mere extension of the animal kingdom; he is special, he stands out from the rest of God's creation. In Genesis 1:27, we encounter three parallel clauses celebrating the creation of man:

> And God created man in His own image,
> in the image of God He created him;
> male and female He created them.

Through Hebraic parallelism, the author accents man's creation in God's image, and the high status that image confers upon man. Lines one and two echo each other, and the third line expands upon the first two, clarifying that both sexes bear the image of God.

Clearly, then, the "image of God" concept is crucial for a Christian understanding of man. But what is the nature of this image? Did the fall affect it? If so, does Christ restore it? Unfortunately, theologians have argued for years about such questions, to no avail. The reason for this is simple. Nowhere does Scripture describe the image of God in a clear way.

Traditionally, many have sought to locate God's image in some substantial "faculty" of man, such as the size of his brain, his reason, will, or imagination. Others have interpreted it not as some capacity of man, but as man in his relation to God and in his reflection of God's will. Emil Brunner sought to bring both these interpretations together in his distinction between the "formal" *imago Dei* (capacities such as will and reason), and the "material" *imago Dei* (relationship with God).[3]

But the more we study scriptural terms such as *soul*, *body*, *spirit*, and *image of God*, the more we realize that the Hebrews' purpose was not to satisfy esoteric speculations about the intrinsic nature of man or his parts. Curiosity about the nature of things is more in keeping with Greek thought. The Hebrews were concerned with the *results* of the granting of this image, what the *imago Dei* does to man and for man.

For this reason, we may disagree to some extent as to the exact nature of God's image in man. (Quite likely, the image of God encompasses man as a whole, rather than some combination of parts or faculties, and pertains primarily to man's moral and spiritual relationship to God.) But more important is the truth that God's image belongs by nature to man as man, both as created and as fallen, simply because God made him that way. That is, Scripture portrays this image as designating the essential nature of man, something that is *inherent* or *intrinsic* in man's being. Nor did man lose it through the fall; to do so he would have ceased being man!

Nor is the divine image something now to be earned or accomplished by man; it is a given, by God. This is precisely where D. Gareth Jones goes astray in *Brave New People*. For Jones, the image of God refers to "God-like attributes" that enable us to relate intimately with God. The ability to communicate, to relate, to make choices, to possess self-awareness, and to desire loving and meaningful relationships are all needed, he says. Thus, a fetus is only a "potential person" until "it will in time *demonstrate* these characteristics of personhood" (italics mine).[4]

But the Christian cannot say the image of God depends on what someone can demonstrate! The Bible never speaks of a man becoming or attaining God's image. Man *bears* God's image. It is man himself, not some aspect or ability of man, that is made in the image of God. The Bible does not exclude those lacking certain qualities. The handicapped Mephibosheth was cared for and valued by David. The madman "Legion," possessed by a host of demons, received compassion from Jesus.

Paul Ramsay, prominent writer and Christian ethicist, notes that the dignity of man is "an overflow of God's dealing with him," and comes only from the value God has placed on human life. Therefore, it makes no sense for mankind to seek to determine "degrees of relative worth" for human beings.[5]

Similarly, John Frame, professor of systematic theology at Westminster Theological Seminary writes: "The image of God pertains to all aspects of man's being, the physical included. According to Scripture it is man himself, not merely some aspect of man, that is made in the image of God."[6]

The Importance of the Image

Scripture does not clearly reveal what the constitution of the image of God may be. But we can draw certain conclusions from its portrayal of what the image *does* for man.

The narrative surrounding Genesis 1:27 begins by setting mankind *apart from* the rest of creation and bestowing on them an inherent dignity and status:

> Then God said, "Let Us make man in Our image, according to Our likeness; and let them rule over the

fish of the sea and over the birds of the sky and over
the cattle and over all the earth, and over every creep-
ing thing that creeps on the earth" (Genesis 1:26).

Here man is portrayed as the immediate creation of God—
the object of God's special attention and care.[7] This solemn and
divine counsel among the Godhead forms quite a contrast with
the more impersonal commands regarding the rest of creation:

"Let the earth sprout vegetation. . . . Let the waters
teem with swarms of living creatures. . . . Let the
earth bring forth living creatures. . . ." (Genesis
1:11, 20, 24)

God conveys an attitude of deeper personal concern toward man than the rest of creation. By creating man in his own
image, God establishes the basis for our identity and worth.

In Genesis 2, the same contrast between man and the rest
of creation is noticeable. Animals are formed out of the ground
by God (2:9). But in order to make man, God "breathed into his
nostrils the breath of life; and man became a living being" (2:7).

It is clear that the granting of God's image sets man apart
from the rest of creation. But not only is he set *apart from* the
lower orders; he is also set *over* them. Notice in Genesis 1:26
how God mentions in a single breath both man's creation in
God's image and man's dominion over the lower creation. Man
is not only the crown of God's creation, he is also a separate type
of creation. Man is set apart and given supremacy over the animal kingdom and even over earth itself. His mandate is to multiply and fill the earth and to "rule over" all creation. Man is not
simply a higher form of animal life with a greater capacity to
reason. Man is a different form of life altogether.

The Bible clearly sets man apart from the lower creatures.
Yes, both man and beast are animated beings,[8] both have bodies
from the natural order,[9] both may be spoken of as "souls" (Hebrew *nephesh*),[10] and both are blessed to produce seed.[11] But
there is a *qualitative* difference between them. In contrast to the
fish, birds, and beasts, which are mandated only to propagate

after their kind in a form that is their own and bears no image of God, man is copied from his Creator. And he is given many mandates throughout Scripture as he bears this image. His spirit is to know God as Father (Romans 8:15-16); his heart is to be pure and sincere (Matthew 5:8; Hebrews 10:22); his mind is to be set on things of the Spirit (Romans 8:6; Colossians 3:2); his soul is to thirst after God and to wait in silence for him (Psalm 62:1; 63:1); and his body is to be a living and holy sacrifice unto God (Romans 12:1).

Obviously, man has not kept all these mandates. We might ask, then, Did the fall of man destroy the image of God in him? Certainly the fall has affected man: it fractured his original relationship with God and brought evil, death, sickness, and suffering into the perfect universe (Genesis 3:16-24). Surely we may speak of the image of God in man being distorted, for as imperfect beings we have warped the likeness of the holy God.

Yet God, in his grace, allowed us to go on bearing his image. Not to bear it would have meant the end of our existence, for God's likeness is our very essence, as we have seen. Certain passages make it clear that, even after the fall, man still bears the Divine image (1 Corinthians 11:7; James 3:9). In Genesis 9:6 we can see that God still recognizes man's uniqueness, even in a world of sin:

> "Whoever sheds the blood of man,
>   by man shall his blood be shed;
> for in the image of God
> has God made man" (NIV).

In the contemporary world, debate is centered around a definition of personhood based on what a person does. In the Bible, it is by virtue of man's intrinsic nature and his exalted position apart from and over creation—being made in God's image—that humans possess value as persons.

This elevated position of man was clearly understood by David as he contemplated the vast expanse of the heavens one night:

When I consider Thy heavens, the work of Thy
    fingers,
The moon and the stars, which Thou hast ordained;
What is man, that Thou dost take thought of him?
And the son of man, that Thou dost care for him?
Yet Thou hast made him a little lower than God
    [Elohim],
And dost crown him with glory and majesty!
Thou dost make him to rule over the works of Thy
    hands;
Thou hast put all things under his feet,
All sheep and oxen,
And also the beasts of the field,
The birds of the heavens, and the fish of the sea,
Whatever passes through the paths of the seas.
                       (Psalm 8:3-8).

This expression of awe at the value of man granted by God
has been recited by adherents of Judaism and Christianity for
centuries. The Judeo-Christian tradition has always held—at
least until the present day—that *all* men and women are created
in God's image, and that every life is to be considered of value.
It matters not if an individual is young or old, handicapped or
perfectly formed, weak or strong, poor or rich, black or white
or yellow or red. The life of every person is of value to God and
should be to us; until recently, this was unquestionably the
Christian way.

CAN ANYONE BE EXCLUDED FROM PERSONHOOD?

But today many ask the question, Is our tradition right?
Should everyone, without distinction, have a right to live and
be viewed as persons? Perhaps there may be some individuals
who simply do not measure up to the image of God, to full humanness.

The Bible addresses this matter as well. There have always
been groups in danger of losing the right to life—the "weaker"

segments of society, those who cannot defend themselves. They include the poor, children, the handicapped, and the elderly, groups who even now are in danger of losing their personhood status. They have been abused both verbally and physically throughout history.

But the Bible shows clearly the value of all their lives. Each of these groups of people receives special attention in oft-repeated biblical themes: God cares for and defends them; God's law serves to protect them; in the future, justice will prevail for them; and with the coming of Jesus Christ a new dignity and respect has been given to them.

These overriding themes become vitally important as we realize that even today the right to life of these groups is being questioned. True, prochoice advocates would not say, for example, that the poor are not persons. But by stressing the social and economic problems of being born poor and thereby advocating abortion for the poor, the end result is the same. Forms of discrimination today can be very subtle.

The Poor
The issue of poverty is often raised alongside the issue of abortion. People say it is better not to be born than to be born poor. Many think a poor woman must have the right to abort a child she would not be able to care for anyway. Others stress that society cannot afford to pay the welfare costs of poor children. In effect, such arguments must assume that the lives of these children are of no value. Their lack of worth has been determined by how little is in their mother's pocketbook.

The Bible stands in stark contrast. The poor are of great worth to God. He provides for them and defends them. He assures that the poor will be treated with dignity and respect through the Old Testament laws he gave to protect them.[12] Certain laws even provided a new start in life every seventh or fiftieth year so the poor could break out of their cycle of poverty. Clearly, God's response to the poor would be just the opposite of the supposed abortion solution.

In Scripture, the poor were not looked upon in a monolithic way, as though all poor people are poor simply because they are lazy or somehow inferior. The poor included widows, orphans, and strangers, and those who became poor due to fraud, catastrophe, disease—and even for righteousness' sake. Providing for the needs of the poor was evidence of genuine righteousness.

As the nation of Israel grew larger and more affluent, the rich purposely overlooked God's laws and took advantage of the poor. Then the prophets attacked the rich as oppressors of the poor and destitute, and prophesied a future time when God's Servant would bring justice for the poor.[13]

Jesus was that Servant, and he brought new dignity to the poor. Paul tells us that Jesus purposely became poor, that we through his poverty might be made rich (2 Corinthians 8:9). When he arrived in Nazareth, Jesus claimed he had come to "preach the gospel to the poor" (Luke 4:18-21; cf. Isaiah 61:1f.). In parables and teachings, Jesus cited the disparity between the rich and the poor, and told his disciples that they must leave all to follow him.[14] He also warned that the final judgment would be based on how we cared for the poor (Matthew 25:31-46).

So Scripture clearly teaches that the lives of poor people are of value to God. It also teaches that we have a responsibility to provide a truly humane response to the deep problems of the poor. We are not allowed to sidestep this responsibility by eliminating their children. The biblical response is Jesus' response to the poor—true justice, treating the poor with respect, and providing for their needs.

Little Children and the Handicapped

With infanticide on the increase in newborn nurseries, we are well aware that the same terms and logic used to defend abortion are also used to defend infanticide. Proponents argue that the taking of newborn lives is not murder since these little children do not measure up to a definition of person: good mental health, good physical health, ability to socialize, and so on. At present, the value of newly born children is being questioned primarily when the child would prove to be a heavy economic burden or when the child is found to be handicapped. Defenders of infanticide argue that without a certain "quality of life," the future life of these children would be meaningless and not worth living.

Is an infant or little child or handicapped individual less than a person? Certainly they are often treated as less than human beings because their abilities are not as valued as those of adults. But God designates children as a blessing and a gift from him (Psalm 127). He provided protection for children under the Mosaic law (e.g., Leviticus 20:1-5). When children were abused and even sacrificed to idols, the prophets prophesied of Israel's impending judgment from God.[15]

With the coming of Christ, there came a deeper and clearer understanding of the dignity and value of children. Jesus closely identified with the little children, first becoming one of them. Then, when the disciples thought the young children were not important enough to demand Jesus' time and attention, Jesus rebuked the disciples and blessed the children.

When the disciples thought too much of their own importance, Jesus brought a little child into their midst and taught that the kingdom of God belonged to such as these (Matthew 18:1-10). Then he warned them: " 'See that you do not despise one of these little ones, for I say to you, that their angels in heaven continually behold the face of My Father who is in heaven.' " In this way, Jesus sought to assure their protection.

We should be aware that *paidion* (the diminutive form for "child" in Greek) is the term most often used in these contexts. Even the term *brephos* ("infant," "baby," "unborn child") is employed in one of the passages relating the kingdom of God to children (Luke 18:15).

When we ask what Scripture teaches about the handicapped, we are struck by the repeated themes of God's sovereignty and of his assurance of their protection, care, and acceptance. God said: " 'Who has made man's mouth? Or who makes him dumb or deaf, or seeing or blind? Is it not I, the LORD?'" (Exodus 4:11).

The Mosaic Law included provisions for protecting the handicapped.[16] True, under this same Law God distinguished certain of the handicapped from the rest of Jewish society when he excluded them from approaching the altar as priests (Leviticus 21:16-24). For the wholeness of the priest and of the sacrificial lamb served as an outward sign to remind God's people of the need to approach God "without blemish and without spot," and to point to the spotless Lamb of God to come. To take that distinction as an indication that the handicapped are of less worth is to misapply its intention and to misunderstand God's merciful relationship with all his creation.

A point of Job's righteousness was that he was "eyes to the blind, and feet to the lame" (29:15). Ezekiel prophesied against the "shepherds" of Israel, because "those who are sickly you have not strengthened, the diseased you have not healed, the broken you have not bound up . . ." (34:4).

The blind, lame, and deaf figure prominently in prophetic passages. Isaiah tells of a day when

> The eyes of the blind will be opened,
> And the ears of the deaf will be unstopped.
> Then the lame will leap like a deer,
> And the tongue of the dumb will shout for joy
> > (35:5-6; cf. 29:18-19).

Micah envisions a time when the Lord will "'make the lame a remnant,/ And the outcasts a strong nation'" (4:6-7). Zephaniah 3:19 promises:

> "I will save the lame
> And gather the outcast,
> And I will turn their shame into praise and renown
> In all the earth."

The coming of Christ provided a partial fulfillment of these prophecies. Jesus sent as proof to the imprisoned and perplexed

John the Baptist the following word: "The blind receive sight and the lame walk, the lepers are cleansed and the deaf hear, and the dead are raised up, and the poor have the gospel preached to them. And blessed is he who keeps from stumbling over Me" (Matthew 11:5-6). Jesus put much energy into healing the handicapped. We read that he was *moved with compassion* for the leper, for blind Bartimaeus, and for so many others.

Christ's vision of the future was similar to the prophets. He spoke of a future messianic banquet, where the guests turned out to be "the poor and crippled and blind and lame." Therefore, in the present age, he cautioned, "invite the poor, the crippled, the lame, the blind" to your banquet table (Luke 14:13, 21).

Clearly, the same themes employed in Scripture for the poor are used for both the children and the handicapped. God loves and defends them; his law protects them; and with the coming of Christ, a newfound dignity and respect is theirs. Their worth is not based on their abilities or capacities for intelligence. They are people created in God's image who need to know Christ. Infanticide is not the answer.

The Elderly

The philosophy of the euthanasia movement is that some persons are better off dead. A person whose life is judged to be of little or no value may be selected for nontreatment, and perhaps even for active euthanasia. Elderly persons may become burdensome or senile, at which time their personhood may be called into question. Indeed, many elderly people are tempted to regard themselves as of little worth.

Yet in Scripture, a different attitude prevails. Leviticus 19:32 records this command to Israel: "'You shall rise up before the grayheaded, and honor the aged, and you shall revere your God; I am the LORD.'" Honoring the aged and honoring God are placed side by side. Proverbs teaches that "a gray head is a crown of glory," and "the glory of sons is their fathers" (16:31; 17:6). It warns us, "Do not despise your mother when she is old" (23:22). First Timothy 5:1 stands in this same tradition: "Do not sharply rebuke an older man, but rather appeal to him as a father."

At the heart of this approach to the elderly was the fifth commandment: " 'Honor your father and your mother, that your days may be prolonged in the land which the LORD your God gives you" (Exodus 20:12). This was the first commandment with an attached promise (Ephesians 6:2). Thus the old people were venerated and were a mark of the security, prosperity, and wisdom of a society. Zechariah foresees the elderly (and the young) prominent in the coming peace and prosperity of Zion:

> "Old men and old women will again sit in the streets
> of Jerusalem, each man with his staff in his hand be-
> cause of age. And the streets of the city will be filled
> with boys and girls playing in its streets" (8:4-5).

But, as in the case of the poor, the children, and the handicapped, the elderly were also abused in the history of Israel. Micah decries this fact when he writes:

> For son treats father contemptuously,
> Daughter rises up against her mother,
> Daughter-in-law against her mother-in-law;
> A man's enemies are the men of his own household
>
> $\qquad\qquad$ (7:6).

The few examples we have from the life of Christ that treat specifically his relation to the elderly indicate he cared for them as he did for all the weak. Jesus raised the only son of the widow of Nain, and exalted the widow in the temple who gave all she had. He sharply rebuked the religious leaders for circumventing through their traditions the commandment to honor one's father and mother (Mark 7:6-13).

Jesus provided for the care of his own mother on the cross. This example was perhaps in the mind of the apostle Paul when he so strongly commanded: "But if any one does not provide for his own [widowed mother], and especially for those of his household, he has denied the faith, and is worse than an unbeliever" (1 Timothy 5:8). Many elderly widows in Paul's day, apparently, had no one to care for them. So the church provided for their needs (1 Timothy 5:1-16).

The Bible is not unrealistic as it presents the debilitating effects of old age (Ecclesiastes 12:1-7). But the cry of the elderly to God in Psalm 71:9 touches our hearts:

Do not cast me off in the time of old age;
Do not forsake me when my strength fails.

Summary

We conclude, then, that our Judeo-Christian prolife tradition is truly biblical in this way: Within the human race, there are no exceptions to personhood. All people have an equal right to protection. The Bible does not devalue people because they are imperfect according to this world's standards, or because of their status or age. It does not question their right to live. Indeed, God's law protects them, and the coming of Christ served to accent their worth.

This, I believe, is the main reason the evangelical church can never become proabortion. The heavy accent of Scripture on God's care and protection for the weak and defenseless is a theme too strong to bypass.

Is Biological Life Essential to Personhood?

Because the question of biology is so central in the abortion debate, we must divide our response into two parts: what the Bible does not teach and what the Bible does teach about biological life.

The Bible does not teach a *radical separation* between biological life and personhood as defined by prochoice advocates. This comes from a Greek dualistic view of man, not from Scripture.

Greek Dualism

From Plato to the present day, Greek dualism has ruled Western society's view of man. For Plato, the body was the "prison-house of the soul," the unworthy bearer of the soul. Based on this dualism, Aristotle defined man as a "rational animal," the rational soul being infused in the body at the fortieth day for males and the ninetieth day for females. Gnostics regarded the body as material and evil, and ultimately to be discarded; redemption consisted of being set free from the body. (The same was also true of Eastern mysticism—the physical body was evil and the material world an illusion.) More recently, Descartes distinguished between "thinking substances" and "extended substances," which served to carry on this dualistic idea to the present day.

This tendency in society toward a dualistic view of man is evident in prochoice arguments. When Joseph Fletcher identifies rationality as the central criterion of personhood, and writes that one cannot know the abortion issue unless he is able to separate biological life from personhood, he is placing himself in the tradition of Greek thought.[17]

Greek dualism has also invaded the church. Belief in a body-soul dualism has led to a loathing of the body in some branches of Christianity (e.g., monasticism). Theologically, whenever the church debates the timing of the infusion of the soul into the body, it is assuming a dualistic framework more in keeping with Greek thought and Aristotle than with the Bible.

A conservative minister well known for his stand against abortion said recently that we must distinguish between "biological life" and "true human life." In saying this, he was basing his statement on Greek dualism, not the Bible, and was unintentionally aiding the abortion cause.

When we think of a dying person and the use of extraordinary means to keep his body functioning, we might say "the person is gone though the body continues to function through the machine"; or "the sanctity of human life does not include the sanctity of biological life," as though the person is detached from the body. These notions are also borrowed from the Greeks.

Rational Animals

Aristotle's opinion that humans are merely rational animals lies behind the views of many proabortionists. In the theory of evolution, man is said to differ from his primate ancestors only in degree of intelligence. For zoologist Sir Julian Huxley, man's capacity for "conceptual thought" sets him apart from animals. Paleontologist Teilhard de Chardin holds that man has a "better brain." Professor W. H. Thorpe speaks of "the degree of abstraction that can be achieved by man over animal." According to evolutionist ideology, the growth in the size or structure of the brain and the ability to think conceptually mark the difference between man and animals. [18]

The church has embraced this evolutionist way of thinking whenever it has stressed rationality as the central, if not sole, aspect of the image of God. Due to this widespread emphasis, proabortion arguments have made much headway. But intelligence is not God's major prerequisite for determining a person's worth. The size of Adam's brain and his ability to think conceptually did not determine his humanity! Rather, Adam was a soul who was created in God's image so that he might have a personal relationship with God.

If reason is identified with the image of God in man, why do we read in Isaiah 55:8-9: " 'For My thoughts are not your thoughts . . . ' "? Also, why do we find God choosing the "foolish things" of the world to confound the wise? "Not many wise" were chosen (1 Corinthians 1:26-29). God does not seem to place as high a premium on reason as we do.

Contrary to naturalistic evolution, the Scriptures show that man is not just an advanced form of monkey with more intelligence. Whether Christians hold to a literal seven-day creation or allow for long periods of time in God's direction of the development of the earth, on this point all can agree: There is a distinct separation in the creation account between man and animals. The Bible consistently presents man as a special act of creation by the sovereign hand of God. He is made in God's image; there can be no compromise on this truth.[19]

The Biblical View

How does the biblical view of man differ from Greek dualism? According to Scripture, biological life *is* an essential part of a person's being. While body and soul are not synonymous, there is no radical separation between them. Nor is the body evil or ultimately to be discarded. On the contrary,

> Nowhere perhaps is the contrast between Christianity and most other religions more clearly seen than in its insistence in the fact that the body of man is an integral part of him and not merely an accidental and temporary integument.[20]

This psychosomatic unity is possibly best demonstrated in Genesis 2:7, the parallel account of man's creation by God:

> Then the LORD God formed man of dust from the ground, and breathed into his nostrils the breath of life; and man became a living being [soul].

Man (Hebrew: *adam*) is fashioned by God from the dust of the ground (Hebrew: *adamah*). Scholars are not certain that the two words for man and ground come from the same root. But it is no mere coincidence that *adamah* (ground) is used in juxtaposition to *adam* (man) in this single clause. This use is reinforced in Genesis 3:19,

> "Till you return to the ground [adamah],
> Because from it you were taken;
> For you are dust,
> And to dust you shall return."

The opening clause of Genesis 2:7, therefore, accents the physical side of life, man's earthly origin.

Man also has a heavenly origin. The phrase "breath of life" conveys the truth that breath is a manifestation of life, a manifestation derived from the "living God."[21] This belief is seen throughout Scripture. Perhaps the most obvious expression of this faith is Job 34:14-15:

> "If He [God] should determine to do so,
> If He should gather to Himself His
>   spirit and His breath,
> All flesh would perish together,
> And man would return to dust."

Or consider Ecclesiastes 12:7: "Then the dust will return to the earth as it was, and the spirit will return to God who gave it."

The third emphasis, "and man became a living being [soul]," reveals that the combination of God-formed dust (or clay) with the "breath of life" resulted in a "living being [soul]." This indicates to most commentators that man does not have a soul, man *is* a soul.[22] Soul in this context does not refer to a distinct aspect of man, but denotes man's body animated by the breath of God.

With this revelation comes the truth that there can be no radical separation between body and soul, or between biological life and personhood. As Derek Kidner notes in his commentary on Genesis, "although for convenience [man] may be analyzed into two or more constituents," the basic truth here is that "[man] is a unity."[23] A fusion, not a fission, is being taught. Or as George Eldon Ladd affirms:

> Body and the divine breath together make the vital, active *nephesh* (soul). The word [soul] is then extended from the life principle to include the feelings, passions, will, and even the mentality of man. It then comes to be used as a synonym for man himself. Families were numbered as so many souls (Genesis 12:5; 46:27). Incorporeal life for the *nephesh* is never visualized. Death afflicted the *nephesh* (Numbers 23:10) as well as the body.[24]

Even at death, God does not leave men as disembodied spirits. Instead, he states his intention to restore the essential body-soul oneness through the resurrection of the body at Christ's return. In the meantime, it appears that some kind of clothing or "taber-nacle" is provided by God so that the soul "shall not be found naked" (2 Corinthians 5:1-4).[25]

We must realize that the Bible is mute as to a precise defini-tion of *soul*. In fact, psychological terms in Scripture were used in a flexible way. At times, *soul* is used as a synonym for the whole person. At other times, it may refer to the inner life of man as a thinking, willing, understanding being. But we can say with assurance that the Bible confirms the basic unity of man, body, and soul.

Two more truths flow from Genesis 2:7 and are confirmed in the rest of Scripture. First, Genesis 2:7 conveys *a very high view of the body*. For the earth does not bring forth man's body; God puts forth his hand and molds him. Likewise, man does not receive his life from that already found in the world; God breathes directly into man's nostrils in a manner that displays his deep personal interest. We must not be misled to think of man as a mere extension of nature and of the animal kingdom. Genesis 2:7, like Genesis 1:26, reveals the preeminence of man.[26]

This placement of high value on man's biological life per-vades both the Old and New Testaments. The incarnation of Christ and his bodily resurrection provide the foundation for this view. Christ "has sealed human nature with a certificate of value whose validity cannot be disputed."[27] The Christian doctrine of the incarnation includes that the One who came as man (Philip-pians 2:6-8) has now ascended to the right hand of God without ceasing to be man.

Paul's aim is to magnify Christ *in his body* (Philippians 1:20). He notes that the Christian has the privilege in life of "al-ways carrying about in the body the dying of Jesus, that the life of Jesus also may be manifested in our body" (2 Corinthians 4:10). When dealing with the question of immorality among Christians, Paul reminds them that "the body is not for immoral-ity, but for the Lord; and the Lord is for the body." For the "body is a temple of the Holy Spirit. . . . therefore glorify God in your body." (1 Corinthians 6:13, 19-20).

While the body has been affected by sin and can be spoken of as "the body of this death," Paul also speaks of the renewal of the body and its members in the lives of those in Christ Jesus. Therefore we are to present our "members" as instruments of righteousness to God (Romans 6:12-14), and our "bodies" as a living and holy sacrifice (Romans 12:1). The Bible looks forward to a resurrection of the body, and even to a new spiritual body. For this reason, in Christian tradition, we respectfully bury the body. In contrast, Eastern religions cremate the body as a worthless cast-off. Also, the bodies of aborted babies today are cremated, put down the disposal, or discarded with the trash, in line with the philosophy that the bodies have no value.

Second, Genesis 2:7 conveys *a very high view of life*. We are reminded that proabortionists have their own definition of life. Life, for them, is mere biological life and has no real relation to personhood.

But in Scripture, the term *life* describes the very essence of man. As we read in 2:7: "[God] breathed into his nostrils the breath of *life*, and man became a *living* being." God is the source of life, and true life consists in having God as "my portion forever" (Psalm 73:26). Life is grounded in Jesus Christ who became a life-giving spirit, and is able to give life to the world.[28] In the New Testament, life is associated with light, glory, honor, immortality, resurrection, eternal life, holiness, joy, spirit, and the imperishable. Life is also associated with the body; it has to do with the whole man![29] Such lofty and true concepts become trivialized in abortion rhetoric that speaks of someone having to reach a certain "quality of life" in order to be of value.

We have worn out the subject, and purposely so; yet we have only touched the surface. Nevertheless, we can conclude with certainty that because of the Bible's high regard for the biological dimension of life and because of the fundamental unity of the whole man, body *and* soul, the prochoice idea that biological life is irrelevant to a definition of personhood is totally foreign to Scripture. Yet this dualism is a basic presupposition of prochoice logic. Without this separation of the physical from personhood in their thinking, the idea of development toward personhood makes no sense. The biological facts would speak for themselves as to who is human.

DOES SCRIPTURE PLACE AN ABSOLUTE VALUE ON HUMAN LIFE?

Some suppose that Scripture does not place an absolute value on human life. They recite passages in which Old Testament Law allows for the taking of life in certain circumstances (when a person is pronounced guilty of a crime, or in the defense of one's life, or in war.) Therefore, says D. Gareth Jones, there is no "absolute" value on human life:

> If that is the case the fetus does not have an unqualified right to protection. Our view of the fetus should be a high one, but it should not be an absolute one. The fetus, being weak and defenseless, should receive considerable protection, but that is not the same as guaranteeing absolute protection.[30]

The conclusion drawn by Jones is hardly warranted by the evidence that Scripture allows for the taking of human life in certain circumstances. For where the taking of human life is permitted in Scripture, the one whose life is taken is guilty of some *capital offense*. Is Jones contending that a fetus is somehow guilty of a capital offense?

Surely not. The fetus is innocent of any capital crime. So the question becomes, Does innocent human life have an unqualified right to protection? To this question, the Scripture gives a resounding affirmative response.

Innocent Blood

It isn't long after the accounts of the creation and the Fall that the Bible introduces us to acts of violence. First came Cain, who slew his brother Abel. God's defense of the innocent dead is clear: "'The voice of your brother's blood is crying to Me from the ground'" (Genesis 4:l0). Thus begins the biblical theme of innocent blood polluting the land:

> "So you shall not pollute the land in which you are; for blood pollutes the land and no expiation can be made for the land for the blood that is shed on it, except by the blood of him who shed it" (Numbers 35:33).

God had charged Israel, before they entered the promised land: "'Do not kill the innocent or the righteous, for I will not acquit the guilty'" (Exodus 23:7). In Deuteronomy 21:1-9, a provision was even given to cover the sin of an unknown murderer's crime. If a slain person is found in an open field, then the nearest city shall kill a heifer and wash their hands over the heifer, and pray:

> "Forgive Thy people Israel whom Thou hast redeemed, O LORD, and do not place the guilt of innocent blood in the midst of Thy people Israel" (v. 8).

In this way the guilt of the "innocent blood" was removed from their midst, and they were forgiven.

The book of Proverbs begins:

> My son, if sinners entice you,
> Do not consent.
> If they say, "Come with us,
> Let us lie in wait for blood,
> Let us ambush the innocent without cause;
> ....
> My son, do not walk in the way with them.
> Keep your feet from their path,
> For their feet run to evil,
> And they hasten to shed blood.
> ....
> But they lie in wait for their own blood;
> They ambush their own lives.

> So are the ways of everyone who gains by violence;
> It takes away the life of its possessors
> > (Proverbs 1:10-11, 15-16, 18-19).

Proverbs is filled with such admonitions. To those who permit violence, it warns:

> A man who is laden with the guilt of human blood
> Will be a fugitive until death; let no one support him
> > (28:17).

To those who sit on the sidelines and cheer:

> He who justifies the wicked, and he who condemns
> > the righteous,
> Both of them alike are an abomination to the LORD
> > (17:15).

Yet it appeals to repentance:

> He who conceals his transgressions will not prosper,
> But he who confesses and forsakes them will find
> > compassion (28:13).

Proverbs also puts forth our responsibility:

> Deliver those who are being taken away to death,
> And those who are staggering to slaughter, O hold
> > them back.
> If you say, "See, we did not know this,"
> Does He not consider it who weighs the hearts?
> And does He not know it who keeps your soul?
> And will He not render to man according to his
> > work? (24:11-12).

Seven things God abominates, says Proverbs 6:16-19, and one is "hands that shed innocent blood." In Deuteronomy 27:25, a curse is placed on the one who strikes down an innocent person. Other nations are judged because of their violence in shedding innocent blood (Joel 3:19). Ultimately, the shedding of innocent blood was a major cause for the downfall of Judah:

> Surely at the command of the LORD it came upon
> Judah, to remove them from His sight because of the
> sins of Manasseh, according to all that he had done,
> and also for the innocent blood which he shed, for he
> filled Jerusalem with innocent blood; and the LORD
> would not forgive. (2 Kings 24:3-4)

It can also be the cause of the downfall of a nation today.
God is still the God of the defenseless and the weak. If a nation
permits the slaughter of the innocent, it should expect nothing
less than God's judgment upon itself.[31]

Protection of Life

From Cain and Abel to the Noachic Flood (Genesis 1-6),
widespread sin led to more violence. The Bible notes that God
looked down and saw that the earth was full of violence and that
"every intent of the thoughts of [man's] heart was only evil continually" (Genesis 6:5, 11).

In response, God sent the most severe judgment possible:
the forfeiting of physical life. Desecration of life was judged by
the dissolution of life (6:7). "But Noah found favor in the eyes
of the LORD" because he sought to live righteously in the midst
of that violence.

Following the Flood, God took specific measures to protect human life against such violence. God inaugurated a covenant with Noah intended to enhance and preserve life. Its three
main provisions underlined the safeguarding of human life in
the face of death.

The first provision was for the *propagating* of human life.
God begins as he began with Adam and Eve: " 'Be fruitful and
multiply, and fill the earth' " (9:1).

The second provision was for the *sustaining* of human life.
" 'Every moving thing that is alive shall be food for you; I give
all to you, as I gave the green plant' " (9:3). God also promised
that, until the end of time, nature would keep its course and life
would be sustained (8:22). There would be no more cataclysmic
floods.[32]

The third and central provision of God's covenant with Noah was for *protecting* human life:

> "And surely I will require your lifeblood; from every beast I will require it. And from every man, from every man's brother I will require the life of man.
>   Whoever sheds man's blood,
>   By man his blood shall be shed,
>   For in the image of God
>   He made man" (Genesis 9:5-6)[33]

The rationale behind this provision is clear: "For in the image of God He made man." Again, as in Genesis 1:26, the Divine image serves to give value to human life. One may debate whether the purpose of this heavy penalty was to discourage and inhibit infractions in the future, or was simply understood as the just requirement against such crime. Either way, the *image of God* plays a major role, and the heinousness of the crime is apparent in that the life of the murderer is required.[34]

It is especially significant that *all three provisions* accented in the Noachic covenant are repeated throughout Scripture. So when we examine God's relation to man in Scripture, at least three basic truths emerge:

1. God is the giver of life; he creates life and is intimately involved in the formation and development of it.

2. God sustains life; as Job observes,
       "If He should determine to do so,
         If He should gather to Himself His spirit
           and His breath,
         All flesh would perish together,
         And man would return to dust"
                             (Job 34:14-15).

3. God protects life; the establishment of the death penalty for the murderer demonstrates God's abiding concern for life's protection.

When man takes life into his own hands and acts as though it were his to give and take, he fails to acknowledge that God is still God, and that he is still concerned about violence and the taking of innocent life.

Prohibition against Murder

The third provision of the Noachic covenant is reinforced by the sixth commandment in Exodus 20, "You shall not murder." Many recent commentators try to limit the application of this commandment to its negative side, the prohibition against first-degree murder. But what strikes me is the simplicity and brevity of the command. The Hebrew is an emphatic negative imperative (or prohibition): *lo' tirsah*. The term can refer either to unintentional killing or to intentional murder, though the latter is its more frequent use and no doubt its main use here.

Yet the context of the sixth commandment is general; no one is excluded from its protection. The thrust of the commandment is positive as well as negative—toward protecting the sanctity of all human life, not simply against murder. The entire Mosaic legislation stands against the taking of life, even by carelessness. It even has a law requiring new homes with flat roofs to put a parapet around them, " 'that you may not bring bloodguilt on your house if anyone falls from it' " (Deuteronomy 22:8).

To try to limit the application of the sixth commandment to intentional murder seems pharisaical. For Jesus himself specifically broadened its application in two ways—negatively and positively. Negatively, Jesus warned:

> You have heard that the ancients were told, "You shall not commit murder" and "Whoever commits murder shall be liable to the court." But I say to you that every one who is angry with his brother shall be guilty before the court; and whoever shall say to his brother, "Raca," shall be guilty before the supreme court; and whoever shall say, "You fool," shall be guilty enough to go into the fiery hell (Matthew 5:21-22).

Jesus goes beyond the legal definition of murder by prohibiting thoughts of anger or hatred, which is murder of the heart. For, left to itself, hatred breeds murder.[35] Even worse, says Jesus, is to utter harmful words against those we hate. Such an attack intends to diminish the worth of that person. Our Lord's brother, James, writes that cursing men is a violation of God's will inasmuch as man is made in God's image (James 3:9).

Jesus also positively expanded the scope of the sixth commandment by relating it to the summary: "You shall love your neighbor as yourself" (Matthew 19:18-19; cf. Romans 13:8-10). The love Jesus is speaking of has at least three main characteristics notably absent in much prochoice action:

1. It is selfless, living for others; loving others "as yourself." Paul said we are to imitate God and "walk in love, just as Christ also loved [us], and gave Himself up for us, an offering and a sacrifice. . ." (Ephesians 5:1-2). The unborn are not loved but killed in abortion because of others' unwillingness to sacrifice and care for them.

2. It is directed toward all without exception. Jesus said, "'You have heard that it was said, "You shall love your neighbor, and hate your enemy." But I say to you, Love your enemies. . .'" (Matthew 5:43-44). As in the parable of the good Samaritan, our love is to be extended beyond the bounds of our natural or selfish inclinations.

3. It is in harmony with the law of God. Jesus said, "'If you love Me, you will keep My commandments'" (John 14:15). According to Joseph Fletcher, we are to keep the law of love, and we are to do what love demands in a given situation. But, he says, what love demands is not necessarily what the Bible commands, and to follow its rules without bending is legalism. Our response is that love and law are not

opposites; love does not replace law but enables us to keep the law. John wrote: "For this is the love of God, that we keep His commandments; and His commandments are not burdensome" (1 John 5:3).

We find then that the sixth commandment, rather than being limited to first-degree murder, has in fact a very broad application. Not only is the malicious destruction of life forbidden, but the safeguarding and preserving of life is commanded. Not only are we not to murder or hate or speak abusively against someone else, but we are to love our neighbor sacrificially, without prejudice, and in line with God's commandments. The sixth commandment means not killing but caring.

The Westminster divines, when they raised the following questions in the Westminster Larger Catechism over three hundred years ago, were more in harmony with our Lord's interpretation of the sixth commandment than many of us today:

Catechism #135: What are the duties required in the sixth commandment?
". . . all careful studies, and lawful endeavors, to preserve the life of ourselves and others, by resisting all thoughts and purposes . . . and avoiding all occasions, temptations, and practices, which tend to the unjust taking away the life of any; . . . by charitable thoughts, love, compassion . . . comforting and succoring the distressed, and protecting and defending the innocent."

Catechism #136: What are the sins forbidden in the sixth commandment?
". . . all taking away the life of ourselves, or of others, except in case of public justice, lawful war, or necessary defense; the neglecting or withdrawing the lawful or necessary means of preservation of life; sinful anger, hatred . . . striking, wounding, and whatsoever else tends to the destruction of the life of any."[36]

Is Abortion Murder?

But is abortion murder?

> We seldom refer to abortion as murder (deliberate, premeditated killing) because of the complicating factors involved, such as the mother's stress. But sometimes it offers a surprisingly close parallel: it can be deliberate and premeditated, and it is always killing a human being.[37]

But even putting aside the strict legal definition of murder, it is hard to escape *Jesus'* interpretation of the sixth commandment. His broader application, especially with respect to sacrificial love, stands diametrically opposed to the attitudes and actions surrounding the killing of the unborn. Some would hold that the most loving thing to do to an unwanted child is to abort it. This equates love with the destruction of life, a view hardly in keeping with Jesus. We can only conclude, given Jesus' broader application, that *abortion is the breaking of the sixth commandment*.

We come back then to the introductory question, Does the Bible place an absolute value on human life? If life has an absolute value, *no* considerations could justify the taking of life (thus no capital punishment, self-defense resulting in death, and so on), not even giving up one's own life, as Jesus did. Surely this is not so! But these are matters for other books since this question does not really relate to abortion. The question we should be asking is, *Does innocent life have an unqualified right to protection?* Scripture could not be clearer—it does!

IS DEATH EVER A GOOD ALTERNATIVE?

Granted the high value of human life and the need not to shed innocent blood, can death ever be a viable alternative in a difficult situation? We are not talking here of capital punishment or of war. We are concerned about the bioethical issue of abortion. Our answer will have implications for infanticide and euthanasia as well.

Prochoicers want us to believe that if an unborn child is handicapped or unwanted or will be born into poverty, that child is better off dead. It comes from the growing consensus that suffering is intolerable and death is an acceptable means of escape. Can a Christian justify this point of view? Is the "option of death" a scriptural alternative?

What is Death?

Death, in Scripture, is portrayed as an unwelcome intruder in a world God pronounced to be "very good" (Genesis 1:31). Death was not part of God's original creation, nor was it an inevitable consequence of our physical condition.

Death is not natural! According to John Murray, death is "not the debt of nature, but the penalty of sin."[38] Scripture sets death within the context of willful disobedience, the eating of the forbidden fruit (Genesis 2-3). God had said, "'In the day that you eat from it you shall surely die.'"

While Adam did not experience physical death on the very day he ate, the new reality of sin and guilt were an entrance into a state that inevitably would lead to physical death. The apostle Paul in his commentary on Adam's fall (Romans 5:12-21), insists some six times that the sin which entered the world through Adam was that which brought death upon all. Elsewhere, Paul describes death as the wages of sin, as the consequence of judgment, and as the final enemy to be destroyed.

This last concept is pivotal to our understanding of death. Death is not a welcome friend but an enemy that Jesus Christ came to destroy. The essence of the gospel is that while sin has brought death, redemptive grace found in Jesus Christ has brought life. As Jesus himself said, "'I came that they might have life, and might have it abundantly'" (John 10:10). In this light Paul explains Jesus' resurrection and ascension in 1 Corinthians 15:20-28: "For He must reign until He has put all His enemies under His feet. The last enemy that will be abolished is death" (vv. 25-26).

> Death is not merely the momentary event of dying; it
> is the death state, i.e. Sheol. . . . As a synonym for
> death [Sheol] is the common goal and final leveller
> of all life: man and beast, righteous and wicked, wise
> and foolish. . . . It is a state of sleep, rest, darkness,
> silence, without thought or memory . . . in which
> one does not praise God and from which one does not
> return.[39]

From the entrance of death into the world in Genesis 3 to
the statement in Revelation 21:4 that "there shall no longer be
any death," the themes of life and death run through Scripture as
diametrically opposed goals. God is the creator of life; death is
the forfeiting of the life God created. When God said to Israel
through Moses: " 'I have set before you life and death, the
blessing and the curse' " (Deuteronomy 30:19), he was not
suggesting that death was an acceptable option. He was equat-
ing death with the curse and judgment that comes from sin.

When Paul said, "To live is Christ, and to die is gain"
(Philippians 1:21), he was not supporting the choice to die. Yes,
gain is found in death for the Christian because of Christ's con-
quest of death. The moment we die, we are in his very presence
(1:23). But this does not mean everyone who is "in Christ"
should immediately seek death. The whole tenor of Scripture is
otherwise.

Is Death an Option?

In the midst of all his afflictions, Job was driven to curse
the day he was conceived and born. His wife said, " 'Curse God
and die!' " But Job said, " 'Shall we indeed accept good from
God and not accept adversity?' " (Job 2:9, 10; 3:11ff.) After all
his relatives and friends and servants separated themselves from
him, Job states:

> "I know that my Redeemer [vindicator] lives,
> And at the last He will take His stand on the earth.
> Even after my skin is destroyed,
> Yet from my flesh I shall see God"
> (19:25).

In the Maskil Psalms, where the miseries of this life and the terrors of death are contemplated, the psalmist never asks that his life be taken. Rather, he pleads for deliverance and restoration to life. Even in Psalm 22, with its deep expressions of personal agony and misery, death is neither good nor welcome. The author pleads for redemption.[40]

The essential difference between Scripture and the "option of death" movement is that the Bible says there is hope for deliverance in the face of death. Scripture tells of God's love and care for the afflicted. Since sickness, disease, and death are consequences of the sinful condition of man, every healing was seen as a driving back of death and an invasion of the providence of sin.

With the coming of Christ, the power of God's kingship and reign on earth is evidenced through the miraculous signs he worked. In the New Testament, we often meet extreme injuries or handicaps. Lepers were cleansed; the man born blind received sight; the dead were raised. But even these were temporary healings and resurrections pointing to the ultimate goal of Christ's coming: eternal life in him. They spoke of the direction and purpose of God for life-and-death decisions. God is prolife and antideath, and will ultimately defeat death and provide eternal life in Christ Jesus our Lord.

Of course, even in Scripture, temporary healings and resurrections were not universally available. The apostle Paul, who had healed many in his ministry, had to accept the fact that he himself would not be healed. He had asked the Lord three times to take away the "thorn in the flesh." We are not sure what this was; as a "thorn" it no doubt hurt, and being "in the flesh" probably indicates it was something physical. Paul even referred to it as "a messenger of Satan," as though Satan were the administrator. But Christ said, " 'My grace is sufficient for you, for power is perfected in weakness' " (2 Corinthians 12:9). Paul's hope was not for physical deliverance but for a display of God's power in sustaining him through his trial.

We live in a day when only two alternatives are considered: healing or death. We think, "If I cannot be healed, then I want to die. Suffering is intolerable!" But suffering is, in truth, a clear-cut biblical alternative.

Suffering as an Alternative

The New Testament does not look on suffering as an evil to be avoided at all costs. It can be the means of God working out his purposes in our lives, developing qualities, teaching lessons of his faithfulness and care.

When Christ took the punishment of our sin on himself, his death saved us from our ultimate death. But this does not mean the Christian no longer suffers in this life. Jesus himself said, "'He who does not take his cross and follow after Me is not worthy of Me'" (Matthew 10:38). Paul said, "For to you it has been granted for Christ's sake, *not only* to believe in Him, *but also* to suffer for His sake" (Philippians 1:29).

We are also told that God can have several purposes in suffering. One purpose is to draw men to himself. This theme is found throughout Scripture. In Egypt, Israel cried to the Lord, and he delivered them. In the New Testament, those who suffered were drawn to Jesus for healing. Inevitably, suffering serves this purpose.

Another purpose of suffering is that Christians may bring glory to God. The world always notices the actions of Christians under pressure. Paul is an excellent example of this truth (Philippians 1:12-26). While Paul was in prison, others in the church at Rome were in some way taking advantage of his imprisonment for their own benefit. Moreover, this imprisonment could possibly end in Paul's own death. What purposes of God could any of those problems serve?

Paul's response is, Don't worry about my imprisonment; the gospel is being furthered! Unbelievers are hearing of my being jailed for Christ, and believers are now speaking the Word with more courage. Paul also adds, Don't worry about those proclaiming Christ out of impure motives; the important thing is, Christ is being proclaimed! And don't worry about the possibility of my dying, only that Christ might be glorified in my response in life or in death. Paul's attitude of Christ- centeredness and detachment from attacks and personal suffering is an excellent example for us. The Christian is to live above the circumstances life affords.

An additional purpose of suffering is to make us more like Christ. The author of Hebrews explains that "it is for discipline that you endure." God disciplines us for our own good, "that we may share His holiness." Though "all discipline for the moment seems not to be joyful, but sorrowful; yet to those who have been trained by it, afterwards it yields the peaceful fruit of righteousness" (Hebrews 12:7-11). In addition, the apostle Peter assures us, "after you have suffered for a little while, the God of all grace, who called you to His eternal glory in Christ, will Himself perfect, confirm, strengthen and establish you" (1 Peter 5:10). What more could we ask than to know God is shaping our lives.

The Bible also provides us with several comforting truths. First, Christ understands and sympathizes with our suffering. According to Hebrews, due to the suffering Christ himself experienced, he is able to understand our suffering, to be a source of help, to comfort, and to come to our aid.[41]

Moreover, there is a very special sense, difficult to understand, that our sufferings are intimately related to Christ. When we suffer for righteousness, says Paul, we not only suffer on behalf of Christ, we also share his sufferings.[42] Yet he assures us, God works all things out for good to those who love God (Romans 8:28).

Finally, we realize that our weakness is an opportunity for God to show his grace and power. As he told Paul, " 'My grace is sufficient for you, for power is perfected in weakness.' " So Paul realized, "when I am weak, then I am strong" (2 Corinthians 12:9-10).

There appears to be a principle in Scripture that the kingdom of God is often realized through suffering, that God's power can be perfected in our weakness. This might not be the method we would choose, but it appears to be the method God has chosen—so much so that God gave his only begotten Son to suffer that he might bring many sons into his kingdom.

Returning to the main question, then, death is not an acceptable option in Scripture to escape suffering. God works in a person's life through suffering. This is not to say we should not try to remove suffering any way we can—anesthetics, painkillers, and such. Nor will anything be gained through prolonging inevitable death. But there is much to be lost in promoting the option of death, for while there is life there is hope—hope in Christ's love and power.

Chapter 4, Notes

1. Hebrew: *adam*, *ish*, *nephesh*, *panim*; Greek: *prosopon*, *prosopolepsia* and cognates.

2. *The Compact Edition of the Oxford English Dictionary*, (New York: Oxford University Press, 1971) 2:2140.

3. Emil Brunner, *The Christian Doctrine of Creation and Redemption*, trans. Olive Wyon (Philadelphia: Westminster Press, 1952), 75-78. For reviews of various interpretations, cf. G. C. Berkouwer, *Man: The Image of God*, trans. Dirk Jellema (Grand Rapids: Wm. B. Eerdmans Publishing Co., 1962), 67-118; Paul Ramsay, *Basic Christian Ethics* (New York: Charles Scribner's Sons, 1950), 249ff.

4. D. Gareth Jones, *Brave New People* (Downers Grove, Ill.: Inter-Varsity Press, 1984), 19-21.

5. Paul Ramsay, "The Morality of Abortion," *Life or Death: Ethics and Options* (Seattle: University of Washington Press, 1968), 72f. Similarly, John Jefferson Davis (*Abortion and the Christian: What Every Believer Should Know* [Philadelphia: Presbyterian and Reformed Publishing House, 1984], 36-37) writes: "Man, as *imago Dei*, possessing inalienable dignity and worth, is to be understood not primarily in terms of innate capacities or faculties—whether intellectual, moral, or spiritual—but in terms of his unique relationship to his transcendent Creator and covenant Lord. It is not intrinsic powers of speech, imagination, and rational thought that lend transcendent worth to human nature, but man's unique calling to live in loving fellowship with the triune God for all eternity. Thus there is no place for . . . such criteria as self-awareness, memory, a sense of futurity and time, and a certain minimum I.Q." as Joseph Fletcher has suggested.

6. John Frame, "Abortion from a Biblical Perspective," *Thou Shalt Not Kill*, ed. Richard L. Ganz (New Rochelle: Arlington House, 1978), 46. Cf. Davis, *Abortion and the Christian*, 53-54; Berkouwer, *Man*, 75; Gerhard von Rad, *Old Testament Theology*, trans. D. Stalker (New York: Harper and Row, 1962) 1:145.

7. Some scholars have debated whether image (*tselem*) and likeness (*demuth*) in Genesis 1:26 are referring to the same concept or to two different ideas. This author prefers to view these two terms as referring to the same concept, due to Hebraic parallelism.

8. That animals owe their life to the Spirit of God: Psalm 104:30; cf. Genesis 6:17; 7:15, 22; Ecclesiastes 3:19, 21; Isaiah 31:3.

9. That animals derive their bodies from the ground: Genesis 1:24: "Let the earth bring forth living creatures . . ."

10. That animals are referred to as souls: Genesis 1:24; the word for creatures (see footnote 1) is *nepheshim* (souls).

11. That the seed of animals is blessed to reproduce is not as explicitly stated as in the case of man, but it is still clearly evident: Genesis 1:22-24; 8:17; Deuteronomy 7:12ff.

12. E.g., Deuteronomy 15:1-18.

13. E.g., Micah 2:1ff, 8f; 4:6ff; Isaiah 2:1ff; 5:7ff; 9:6f; 11:1ff. For an overview of this subject, see John Bright, *The Kingdom of God* (Nashville: Abingdon Press, 1953), especially chapters 2 and 3, "A Kingdom Under Judgment" and "A Remnant Shall Return."

14. Luke 12:13ff, 33; 16:19ff.

15. E.g., Jeremiah 19:1ff.

16. E.g., Leviticus 19:14; Deuteronomy 27:18.

17. Joseph Fletcher, *The Ethics of Genetic Control: Ending Reproductive Roulette* (Garden City, N. Y.: Anchor Press, 1974), 133.

18. For a fine discussion and summary of all these views, together with bibliographical information, see Norman Anderson, *Issues of Life and Death* (Downers Grove, Ill.: InterVarsity Press, 1976), 15-16.

19. Applied to the abortion controversy, one can now see why Joseph Fletcher has held that one must have at least an I.Q. of 20 or 40 in order to be a person, and why "rationality" is so high on the list of "quality of life" criteria for proabortionists. They are heavily influenced by naturalistic evolutionary thought. (See Fletcher, as discussed in chapter 2.)

We can also see why those in the prolife movement have a difficult time accepting a definition of brain death, since they so earnestly believe that a person is more than a brain. No wonder abortionists call hydrocephalic children monsters or monkeys, since in their opinion they have not yet graduated to the stage of a "rational animal."

20. E. L. Mascall, *The Importance of Being Human* (London: OUP, 1959), 25.

21. Cf. Bruce K. Waltke, "Reflections from the Old Testament on Abortion," *Journal of the Evangelical Theological Society* 19 (1976):7.

22. Ibid.; Davis, *Abortion and the Christian*, 53f.; Derek Kidner, *Genesis* (London: Tyndale Press, 1967), 50-51. It was H. Weeler Robinson who said: "The Hebrew idea of the personality is an animated body, and not an incarnated soul" (J. A. T. Robinson, *The Body: A Study in Pauline Anthropology* [London: SCM, 1952], 14).

23. Kidner, *Genesis*, 61.

24. George Eldon Ladd, *A Theology of the New Testament* (Grand Rapids: Wm. B. Eerdmans Publishing Co., 1974), 458. A wide range of scholars may be included who hold that man is not to be pictured as a dualistic being, but primarily as a unity: cf. Rudolf Bultmann, *Theology of the New Testament*, trans. Kendrick Grobel (London: SCM Press LTD., 1968) 1:209; D. E. H.

Whiteley, *The Theology of St. Paul* (Oxford: Basil Blackwell, 1970), 31-44; Berkouwer, *Man*, 200-4; D. R. G. Owen, "'Body' and 'Soul' in the New Testament," in *Man's Need and God's Gift*, ed. Millard J. Erickson (Grand Rapids: Baker Book House, 1976), 96.

25. Cf. John Warwick Montgomery, *Slaughter of the Innocents*, (Westchester, Ill.: Crossway Books, 1981), 83-85; also, Oscar Cullmann, *Immortality and Resurrection*, trans. K. Stendahl (New York: Macmillan, 1965), 9-53. It is enlightening to note that while *nephesh* (soul) is regarded as departing at death (Genesis 35:18), the term is never used of the spirit of the dead. *Nephesh* is, however, applied to a dead body (e.g., Leviticus 19:28; Numbers 6:6; Haggai 2:13); cf. Montgomery, *Slaughter of the Innocents*.

26. Cf. Keil and Delitzsch, *Biblical Commentary on the Old Testament*, trans. J. Martin, 10 vols. (Grand Rapids: Wm. B. Eerdmans Publishing Co., n.d.), vol. 1, *The Pentateuch*, 78-80.

27. Mascall, *Being Human*, 22f.

28. 1 Corinthians 15:45; Hebrews 7:16; John 6:33, 63; 2 Corinthians 3:17.

29. Luke 24:39ff; John 5:28f; 1 Corinthians 15; Philippians 3:21; Revelation 20:13. For these and other references as well as for a fine discussion of the term *life*, see E. E. Ellis, "Life," *The New Bible Dictionary*, ed. J. D. Douglas (Grand Rapids: Wm. B. Eerdmans Publishing Co., 1962), 738-39.

30. D. Gareth Jones, "Abortion: Some thoughts on a Perplexing Problem," *Christian Medical Society Journal* 14 (1 November 1983):6.

31. Cf. Harold O. J. Brown, *Death Before Birth* (Nashville: Thomas Nelson Publishing House, 1977), 122.

32. Second Peter 3:3-10 clarifies God's purpose in sustaining and protecting life. The prolonged period between the flood and the future judgment of fire is because God "is patient toward you, not wishing for any to perish but for all to come to repentance" (v. 9).

33. In Genesis 9:2, God had already provided for man's protection from the beast by instilling a fear of man in them. Now he formally stipulates that the life of the beast will be required if it kills a man. We are struck by the contrast with God's original intention for man and beast in Genesis 2:19-20, where there is no sign of fear or dread in the animal towards man, only an apparent submission to man's rule over them. Now, fear and dread is instilled in the animals and man is viewed as needing protection from them. Consistent with this covenant, the Mosaic Law enlarged on this stipulation through case laws by enumerating how an animal that kills a man must be put to death (Leviticus 24:21).

34. Cf. Brown, *Death Before Birth*, 121, n. 4; Davis, *Abortion and the Christian*, 36, 112, n. 1.

35. R. C. Sproul, *Ethics and the Christian* (Wheaton: Tyndale House, 1983), 82.

36. *The Confession of Faith of the Presbyterian Church in the United States* (Richmond, Va.: The Board of Christian Education of the PCUS, 1965), 227-30.

37. Brown, *Death Before Birth*, 118-19, n. 1. For killing to be first-degree murder, malice aforethought must be shown. Perhaps many of those doing the abortions could be seen in this light.

38. John Murray, *Principles of Conduct* (Grand Rapids: Wm. B. Eerdmans Publishing Co., 1978), 107.

39. Ellis, "Life," 736.

40. Scripture has only two examples of euthanasia. Though in both cases the action is not clearly condemned, neither is it approved. When a woman threw an upper millstone on Abimelech's head, thereby crushing his skull, Abimelech asked his armor-bearer to kill him, which he did (Judges 9:50-57). The case is simply recorded by Scripture.

A more significant example involves the death of King Saul. Saul was mortally wounded in battle on Mount Gilboa. Afraid that the enemy would torture him if they found him alive, he pleaded with his armor-bearer to end his life. His armor-bearer refused! Then Saul called upon an Amalekite standing nearby to kill him: "Please stand beside me and kill me; for agony has seized me because my life still lingers in me" (2 Samuel 1:9). He gives the typical reasons for euthanasia. The Amalekite who serves as a neutral observer—neither a Philistine nor a Jew—responds precisely as a practitioner of euthanasia: "So I stood beside him and killed him, because I knew that he could not live after he had fallen" (1:10).

The Amalekite thought he was doing something merciful. But when he came and told David of his merciful action, David responded with severe disapproval: "How is it you were not afraid to stretch out your hand to destroy the LORD's anointed?" (1:14) Some think it was because Saul was the Lord's anointed that David disapproved. Undoubtedly so. But also note the words David uses: "to stretch out your hand to destroy." This description sounds more like an assassination than a mercy killing.

41. Cf. Hebrews 2:14-18; 4:14-16; 5:7-10; 7:26-8:1; 12:1-11; 13:10-14.

42. Philippians 1:29; cf. also 3:10; Colossians 1:24; 2 Corinthians 1:5, 7; 4:10-11; 1 Peter 4:12ff.; 5:8-10; Acts 9:4; Mark 8:34ff.

Chapter 5

What Does Scripture Say about the Unborn?

*I*n our discussion of the biblical view of personhood thus far, we have found that all human life, from the point of birth on, is of value before God. But another question must be raised for us to address the abortion issue: Does the value of human life extend to life before birth, even back to conception? More specifically: When does human life begin? Are there any passages that might indicate life in the womb is of less value than life after birth? How does Scripture view development in the womb?

Some believe Scripture cannot or does not address these questions. I disagree. Scripture is full of references and themes relating to the unborn. In the following section, we'll survey some of these references and examine their contribution to the abortion debate.

WHEN DOES HUMAN LIFE BEGIN?

While prochoice advocates try to make light of the significance of conception and deny it as the crucial moment that begins a human life, Scripture places a high importance on conception.

136 What Does Scripture Say about the Unborn?

Of course, a major source for the idea of conception as the start of new life is the scriptural account of the birth of Jesus. The angel Gabriel, when explaining the process to the Virgin Mary, said: "'Behold, you will conceive in your womb, and bear a son, and you shall name Him Jesus'" (Luke 1:31). One can hardly speculate about Jesus' life, as to whether it began at the first heartbeat, quickening, viability, or birth. The angel messenger clearly announces the life of the Savior beginning with conception. Was there a period of time between conception and when he became a *person*? I think not! Some might argue that Jesus' incarnation is unique and cannot be made the norm for the biblical view of conception. But it fits in naturally and reasonably with all the other passages we will consider.

We might ask, Did the biblical writers and the people living then really understand conception that clearly? After all, it has only been since the early nineteenth century that science has discovered what takes place biologically during conception. Moreover, the Bible is not a textbook on biology. What did the ancients understand about conception?

Obviously, people in biblical times did not have the benefit of modern biology. But they did have a basic understanding of the processes of conception and pregnancy as well as birth. The prophetic curse on Ephraim follows the process of life back to its origin:

As for Ephraim, their glory will fly away like a
    bird—
No *birth*, no *pregnancy*, and no *conception*!"
                                            (Hosea 9:11)

Some forty times Scripture refers to conception as the start of new life in the womb of the mother. In the Genesis narratives alone, the phrase "conceived and bore" is found eleven times. The close pairing of the two words clearly emphasizes conception, not birth, as the starting point of life.[1]

We also find *conception* used metaphorically in Scripture to refer to the origins of thoughts or purposes (Isaiah 59:13; Acts 5:4; Psalm 7:14; James 1:15). James 1:15, for example, carries the figure out in detail: "Then when lust has *conceived*, it gives *birth* to sin; and when sin is accomplished, it brings forth *death*." It is obvious in James's metaphor that he considered conception the beginning of the matter, the crux or origin.[2]

What did the people of biblical times know about concepts such as the uniting of ovum and sperm? The biblical writers understood the woman's womb as the place for the protection and growth of the child. Since the idea of a woman's *ovum* or *egg* is never mentioned by the biblical writers, I doubt they knew ova existed. But *seed* is a common term, the "seed" understood as flowing from a man during intercourse to cause conception. For example, Onan knew that spilling his seed on the ground would prevent conception (Genesis 38:9). The idea of seed is also used metaphorically in both testaments to denote physical or spiritual descendants.[3]

The biblical writers never say the words, "Life begins at conception." But they consistently refer to conception as the starting point of a person's life, or metaphorically of the life of an idea. The usage is consistent throughout Scripture, even with its many writers extending over a period of some fifteen hundred years.

Closely aligned to conception as the beginning of life is the view that life is passed on seminally, seed coming to fruition generation after generation. After the fall, the first great promise of redemption is given—Eve's *seed* would ultimately triumph over the seed of the Serpent:

"And I will put enmity
Between you and the woman,
And between your seed and her seed;
He shall bruise you on the head,
And you shall bruise him on the heel"

(Genesis 3:15).

God's plan referred not just to a coming child, or even the conception of the child, but the seed that would cause the conception. And God's promise of a redemptive seed enhanced the sanctity of life in the womb. There followed more seed promises to

Abraham and to his posterity. God promised David that through his *seed* an everlasting kingdom would be established (2 Samuel 7:12-16).

In Isaiah 7:14 the Messianic prophecy is given: "'Behold, a virgin will be with child and bear a son, and she will call His name Immanuel.'" Matthew and Luke show that the seed of the redemptive line culminates in Christ.

The seed, of course, is only one part of conception. Though the Bible never mentions the ovum, part of God's covenant blessing to women consisted in their being fruitful. The promise of children is part of God's blessing for faithfulness on Israel's part. At Mount Sinai, God promised to bless the nation with conceptions and live births if they would remain faithful:

> "But you shall serve the LORD your God, and He will bless your bread and your water; and I will remove sickness from your midst. There shall be no one miscarrying or barren in your land; I will fulfill the number of your days" (Exodus 23:25-26; cf. Deuteronomy 7:13-15).

It is in this context that several related biblical themes should be viewed. First, God is portrayed as active in the event of conception itself. Examples abound, as in the case of Ruth: "The LORD enabled her to conceive, and she gave birth to a son" (Ruth 4:13). And there is Hannah who, after praying for a child, conceives and gives birth: "And she named him Samuel, saying, 'Because I have asked him of the LORD'" (1 Samuel 1:20).

The idea that God opens the womb and gives life at conception is a fundamental belief in Genesis 12-50, where we follow the slender line of succession of the promised seed to the twelve sons of Jacob. Sarah, Rebekah, and Rachel were all barren and distraught, frustrated at their inability to bear children. Genesis is the story of how God provided them a seed and enabled them to conceive, thereby fulfilling his covenant promises to Abraham.[4]

The belief that conception is a gift from God and a fulfillment of his covenant promises continued throughout the life of the people of Israel. This gift concept is beautifully expressed in the Psalms:

> Behold, children are a gift of the LORD;
> The fruit of the womb is a reward.
> Like arrows in the hand of a warrior,
> So are the children of one's youth.
> How blessed is the man whose quiver is full of them
>
> (127:3-5a).
>
> Your wife shall be like a fruitful vine,
> Within your house,
> Your children like olive plants
> Around your table.
> Behold, for thus shall the man be blessed
> Who fears the LORD
>
> (128:3-4).

Concerning the golden age to come, Jeremiah suggests the divine ideal will be: "'Behold, days are coming,' declares the LORD, 'when I will sow the house of Israel and the house of Judah with the *seed* of man. . .'" (31:27).[5]

Are all these references about the importance and preciousness of children saying, therefore, that each life is an immediate act of creation by God? I don't believe so (except, of course, in the overshadowing of Mary by the Holy Spirit in the conception of Jesus). It would appear that in Genesis 1:28 God instituted the process of human reproduction, and in Genesis 2:2 he ceased from his work of creation. No longer does God create biological life from the dust, as he did Adam. Paul taught in Acts 17:26 the solidarity of the human race: "'[God] made from one, every nation of mankind to live on all the face of the earth.'"

On the other hand, this natural human process of procreation does not rule out the truth that God can still be active even in conception, and "open the womb" and give life. God continues actively to guide and sustain all of life according to his holy will. Biblical passages revealing the divine role in conception simply serve to confirm that it is more than just a biological phenomenon. The start of a human life is clearly a special occurrence in which God takes part.

Knowing the role God plays in conception, we might ask whether abortion could ever be legitimate from a Christian perspective. Does not abortion deny the holy nature of conception, the divine opening of the womb? Does not the attempt to undervalue the importance of conception for the beginning of human life go contrary to the clear teaching of Scripture? And does not the contemporary attitude toward the unborn as an inconvenience or burden fly directly in the face of their being a blessing from God?[6]

WHAT VALUE DOES GOD PLACE ON UNBORN LIFE?

That the Bible shows life begins at conception raises an even more important issue: What value does Scripture place upon human life once it has been conceived? Certainly it is a high value—but how high? The value of the unborn in Scripture may be studied in several ways: by their relation to the image of God, by their relation to God, by their continuity with postnatal life, and by the views about their untimely death.

Their Relation to the Image of God

Several verses assume explicitly or implicitly that the fetus is made in God's image. Genesis 5:3 reads: "When Adam had lived one hundred and thirty years, he became the father of a son in his own likeness, according to his image, and named him Seth." Most commentators interpret the phrases, "in his own likeness, according to his image," as meaning the image of God. The Hebrew verb *Yalad*, rendered here "became the father of," is often translated "begot." The verb's primary meaning is "to bear" or "to bring forth children." However, verbs have different forms in Hebrew, and the verbal form in this verse is the causal form. We could translate it literally, Adam "caused to bring forth" Seth, the cause being sexual intercourse and the resulting conception.

If this translation is correct, then Adam and Eve were the only ones literally created in God's image. Seth (and all other descendants of Adam and Eve) received the image of God through procreation. Seth's essential humanness was already present at conception.[7]

The presence of the image of God may also be assumed when the Bible refers to the sinful nature of the unborn. For if the unborn can be shown to have a moral nature, would this not be evidence in favor of their being in the image of God? The verse most often recited in this regard is Psalm 51:5. In repentance over his sin with Bathsheba, David laments:

> Behold, I was brought forth in iniquity,
> And in sin did my mother conceive me.

This certainly supports the notion that man already bears God's image—marred by sin—from conception on.[8]

Other passages supporting the sinful, and hence moral, nature of the fetus include Psalm 58:3:

> The wicked are estranged from the womb;
> These who speak lies go astray from birth [literally:
>   from the womb].

Job suggests the same thing:

> "Who can make the clean out of the unclean?
> No one!"

Eliphaz then concurs:

> "What is man, that he should be pure,
> Or he who is born of a woman, that he should
>   be righteous?"
>   (Job 14:4; 15:14; cf. 25:4).

To these verses we could add the human solidarity in Adam's sin (Romans 5:12ff.). Biblical theologian George Ladd writes: "It is quite clear that Paul believed in 'original sin' in the sense that Adam's sin constituted all men sinners."[9] The entire human race, including the unborn, share in a sphere of existence that is moral in nature, and since the Fall is characterized by sin.

Putting all this together, we may conclude that man's moral, spiritual faculty is already present in the fetus before birth. If the image of God pertains to man's moral nature, then that nature has been passed on from Adam (Genesis 5:3). It is hard to argue that someone is not a person who has moral attributes.

In addition to the image of God and moral attributes, we find certain personality traits attributed to the fetus in utero. Jacob and Esau "struggled together" in Rebekah's womb prior to birth. John the Baptist was said to be "filled with the Holy Spirit" while still in his mother's womb. He "leaped for joy" upon the arrival of Mary with Jesus in her womb. Though these references to personality in utero are few, they do support the thesis that the unborn are persons.

In fact, we may summarize our evidence this way. We accept that Scripture does not provide a precise definition of the soul. It is also mute as to when a body acquires a soul. While some are ready to postulate that the unborn do not yet have souls, they have to do so apart from Scripture. It may be that we cannot prove to everyone's satisfaction that the unborn are souls from conception, but we do know the following from Scripture:

1. The unborn are alive and growing from conception, and are human;
2. Conception and growth are important to God;
3. The "soul" can, on the one hand, refer to man as a whole being; on the other hand to the inner life of man as a thinking, willing, understanding person, and thus as a moral agent;
4. Scripture appears to teach that the image of God is passed on seminally after Adam and Eve;
5. The imputation of the guilt of sin can only happen to a moral agent—not to a body without a soul; and
6. The rejoicing of John the Baptist in the womb is an indication of "soul-presence" since feelings and the will were involved.

So the burden of proof lies on the view that the unborn child acquires a soul at some later point in pregnancy or childhood, which view is also aligning itself with classical Greek thought, not Scripture.

Their Relation to God

The relationship of God to the fetus is significant.

> If God relates in a personal way to a human creature, this is evidence that that creature is made in God's image. And it is abundantly evident from Scripture that God relates to us and is personally concerned for us before birth. [10]

Scripture shows God relating to the fetus in several intimate ways. First, a number of references concur that God oversees the development of the fetus. Job teaches (31:13-15) that God not only made him in the womb, but also fashioned everyone, including Job's slaves. The psalmist acknowledges: "Thy hands made me and fashioned me" (119:73). David reflects on the amazing way God "knit" his body "in the secret place" (Psalm 139:13-16). Jeremiah reports what the Lord had said to him:

> "Before I formed you in the womb I knew you,
> And before you were born I consecrated you"
>
> (1:5)

A second way God relates personally to the unborn is preparing them as individuals for a specific calling. Jacob was given preeminence over Esau, though "not yet born" (Romans 9:11). Samson's mother was told not to eat anything unclean nor to drink wine or strong drink while pregnant, " 'for the boy shall be a Nazirite to God from the womb; and he shall begin to deliver Israel from the hands of the Philistines' " (Judges 13:3-5). God knew Jeremiah even before he was conceived and consecrated him while in the womb (Jeremiah 1:5). Paul writes that God had set him apart, even "from my mother's womb" (Galatians 1:15). Other examples could be cited. Clearly, life in the womb is a stage in the realization of God's plan for an individual.

God's concern and active involvement in the progress of the unborn differs strongly from the proabortionist's dismissal of the unborn as worthless nonpersons. John Davis summarizes the Bible passages well when he writes:

> All these texts indicate that God's special dealings with human beings can long precede their awareness of a personal relationship with God. God deals with human beings in an intensely personal way long before society is accustomed to treat them as persons in the "whole sense.". . . God's actions present a striking contrast to current notions of personhood.[11]

God's personal involvement with the unborn provides the foundation for their personal worth. If we are persons because God has related to us in a personal way, then the unborn are also persons since God's care for them obviously begins in the womb.

Continuity with Life after Birth

A third way Scripture indicates the fetus's value is that a significant continuity between prenatal and postnatal human life is assumed. David sees *himself* as having existed in his mother's womb (Psalm 139:13ff.). The nativity narratives concerning John the Baptist and Jesus unmistakably point to a continuity between pre- and postbirth. Every time we read passages such as Genesis 21:2-3—"So Sarah conceived and bore a son to Abraham. . . . And Abraham called the name of his son who was born to him . . . Isaac"—a personal continuity is assumed from conception through birth to a named individual.

The biblical writers did not use different words to label prenatal and postnatal life. The same Hebrew and Greek terms are often used to refer both to the born and the unborn. For example, *Geber* is a Hebrew noun usually translated man, male, or husband. In Job 3:3, Job curses the night in which it was said, "a man-child [*geber*] is conceived." *Yeled* is a term in Hebrew commonly translated child or boy. Yet Genesis 25:22 refers to *yeladim* (children) struggling inside the womb of Rebekah. Moses recites a law in which a *Yeled* (child, boy) comes forth from a woman (born prematurely).

In Greek, *brephos* is often used of infants and the newly born (Luke 18:15; 1 Peter 2:2; Acts 7:19). But in Luke 1:41 and 44, *brephos* is used of John the Baptist leaping in the womb of Elizabeth. *Huios* in the Greek means son and is used in Luke 1:36 of John being conceived by Elizabeth: " 'And behold, even your relative Elizabeth has also conceived a son in her old age; and she who was called barren is now in her sixth month.' "

The Bible commonly applies personal language to the unborn. Hosea comments on how, in the womb, Jacob took "his brother" by the heel (12:3). The personal pronouns *me, my,* and *I* are regularly used by writers referring to their lives before birth.[12] Some scholars claim this does not mean much since most people use personal pronouns as a normal way of speaking. However, this manner of speaking of life in utero at the very least warns us against making a sharp separation between the pre-and postnatal periods in our lives for the purpose of demeaning the value of the unborn.

Their Untimely Death

A fourth, though negative, way of ascertaining the value of the unborn is to look at Scripture's view of their "untimely death." We have seen how conception and birth were viewed as wonderful blessings from the Lord. The opposite was also true; miscarriages and murders of the unborn (pregnant women being ripped open) were viewed as a dreadful curse for any people. These themes are highly visible throughout Scripture.

Hazael, future king of Aram, asked Elisha why he wept for him. Elisha replied: " 'Because I know the evil that you will do to the sons of Israel: their strongholds you will set on fire, and their young men you will kill with the sword, and their little ones you will dash in pieces, and their women with child you will rip up' " (2 Kings 8:12). It was Amos who prophesied against the sons of Ammon that they would surely be punished "because they ripped open the pregnant women of Gilead/ In order to enlarge their borders" (Amos 1:13). The "ripping open of pregnant women" killed both child and mother.

The untimely death of the unborn or newly born is often recalled to picture the curse of God upon a people due to their unrighteousness. In a gruesome prophecy, Hosea declared that due to Israel's sins, God would close the nation's wombs. Then he continued:

> Give them, O LORD—what wilt Thou give?
> Give them a miscarrying womb and dry breasts.
> . . . .
> Ephraim is stricken, their root is dried up,
> They will bear no fruit.
> Even though they bear children,
> I will slay the precious ones of their womb.
> . . . .
> Samaria will be held guilty,
> For she has rebelled against her God.
> They will fall by the sword,
> Their little ones will be dashed in pieces,
> And their pregnant women will be ripped open
> (Hosea 9:14, 16; 13:16).

Because these passages refer to miscarriages and the ripping open of pregnant women as the ultimate form of punishment for sin and as a sign of a dreadful curse, it is not difficult to see why abortion was so alien to the Hebrew mind. In their world and life view, there was no place for abortion or the destruction of life in the womb. No doubt this is why abortion is not discussed in Scripture. There was no need for a prohibition against feticide any more than against uxoricide (wife-killing); both were covered by the sixth commandment against homicide, "You shall not murder" (Exodus 20:13).

When we apply these texts to our times, it is clear that it is quite a responsibility to make a decision to abort one's own child. Such an action deliberately brings on one's own family the fate which in Scripture is the symbol of divine curse! Conversely, the decision to care for the "precious ones" of the womb (Hosea 9:16) is in character with the purposes and desires of God.

ARE THERE ANY PASSAGES THAT DEVALUE THE UNBORN?

According to John Frame, "There is *nothing* in Scripture that even remotely suggests that the unborn child is anything less than a human person from the moment of conception."[13] The only passage sometimes used to argue that the life of a fetus is not as valuable as that of the mother is Exodus 21:22-25. But there are several interpretations of this passage, and a brief survey of them will clarify the issue.

One interpretation is reflected in the New American Standard Bible:

> (22) "And if men struggle with each other and strike a woman with child so that she has a miscarriage, yet there is no further injury, he shall surely be fined as the woman's husband may demand of him; and he shall pay as the judges decide. (23) But if there is any further injury, then you shall appoint as a penalty life for life, (24) eye for eye, tooth for tooth, hand for hand, foot for foot, (25) burn for burn, wound for wound, bruise for bruise."

This translation views the child as having died of a miscarriage. The reference to "no harm" refers only to the woman. The penalty is not very severe, only a monetary exchange, determined perhaps by the age of the fetus or consideration of the loss of a son or daughter. Verses 23-25 then refer to possible harm incurred by the mother, in addition to the miscarriage. If some serious injury befalls the mother, then the more serious *lex talionis* ("eye for eye") principle is brought to bear on the case.

Some interpreters accept this translation of the passage and do not see that it affects one's view of abortion.[14] Others, however, who rely on this translation interpret it to mean that the life of the mother is of more value than the life of the fetus, due to the more serious penalty prescribed for harm to the mother. If the fetus is of less value than the mother, it follows that serious concerns of mothers today may have to take priority over the life of their unborn children. Circumstances in the mother's life (such as trauma from rape or incest, the knowledge that the child to be born is deformed, the mother's own physical or mental well-being, and so on) may then justify aborting the child for the mother's well-being.

One problem with this view is that it is based on a faulty translation. A second interpretation of this passage exposes the errors in translation. A more exact rendering of the Hebrew is found in the New International Version:

> (22) "If men who are fighting hit a pregnant woman and she gives birth prematurely but there is no serious injury, the offender must be fined whatever the woman's husband demands and the court allows.
> (23) But if there is serious injury, you are to take life for life, eye for eye . . ."

According to this second interpretation, the child is born prematurely, but *does not die*. No serious harm occurs to the mother or child, only some trauma or less serious affects, so the monetary requirement is proper. In verse 23, the serious harm can refer to either the mother or the child or both, and in this case the *lex talionis* principle is proper.[15]

There are several good reasons the second interpretation is to be preferred. First, the literal translation of verse 22 is: "so that the child depart." This cannot refer to a miscarriage. The word normally used for miscarriage in Hebrew is *shakol* and is used in a passage as nearby as Exodus 23:26. The verb here is *yatza*, meaning "to go or come forth." It is used elsewhere in Scripture to describe normal births and never refers to a miscarriage. The Hebrew word for child (*yeled*) is always used of someone already born (with the exception of Esau and Jacob in Genesis 25:22), and is usually translated as "child" or "boy."[16] There are Hebrew words for fetus (*golem*) or for the death of an unborn child (*nefel*), usually translated "one untimely born."

But these words are not found in these verses. Moreover, where the NASB reads, "if there is no further injury," as though there had been a miscarriage to the child but no injury to the mother, we find *further* is not even in the Hebrew. The Hebrew simply means injury, or possibly, serious injury.

I believe, therefore, this second interpretation is more accurate than the first. A third interpretation has also been made, which concludes that the mother is killed in the attack mentioned in Exodus and that the child may also be injured or die, with appropriate punishment meted out to the offenders. The accuracy and detail of this interpretation (made by Meredith G. Kline of Gordon Conwell Theological Seminary) is impressive but complex, so I will not go into it here. [17] At the crucial point, it agrees with the second interpretation: this Exodus text is not speaking of a miscarriage but of a premature live birth. And the value of the fetus is being stressed in this passage, not denied.

HOW DOES SCRIPTURE VIEW DEVELOPMENT IN THE WOMB?

Scripture's view of the value of prenatal life has already been resolved, I believe, in our discussion above. God plays an active role at conception. But Scripture also shows his involvement in the development of the child in utero. Quite clearly, as John Stott says:

> The fetus is not a growth in the mother's body (which can be removed as readily as her tonsils or appendix), nor even a potential human being, but a human life who, though not yet mature, has the potentiality to grow into the fullness of the humanity he already possesses. [18]

Stott arrives at this point of view by looking in particular at what many regard as the Bible's *locus classicus* on the development of life in the womb, Psalm 139:13-16. This is a wonderful passage set within a very significant context, and merits our careful consideration:

(13) For Thou didst form my inward parts;
    Thou didst weave me in my mother's womb.
(14) I will give thanks to Thee, for I am fearfully and
        wonderfully made;
    Wonderful are Thy works,
    And my soul knows it very well.
(15) My frame was not hidden from Thee,
    When I was made in secret,
    And skillfully wrought in the depths of the earth.
(16) Thine eyes have seen my unformed substance;
    And in Thy book they were all written,
    The days that were ordained for me,
    When as yet there was not one of them.

These verses express the scriptural view of God's intimate involvement in development in the womb. Certain scholars object to their use pertaining to the abortion issue because the passage is poetic and not to be taken literally. Such an objection, however, betrays a shallow understanding of literature in general and poetry in particular.

Metaphor is a common tool of the poet. A metaphor is a sort of analogy to help the reader feel the truth the poet wishes to express. The Psalms contain many examples of metaphor. Of course no one takes Psalm 23 to mean literally that God is a shepherd who wishes his people to recline in the grass! Neither does anyone call the psalmist a liar for referring to God as a shepherd. The metaphor brings home the truth of God's care for his children in daily circumstances and in times of distress and danger.

Likewise, no one would claim that Psalm 139 really means that God weaves on a loom, sees with physical eyes, or writes in a literal book. But use of metaphor does not belie the truth behind the poem. Rather, the psalmist's poetic expression makes the truth hit home more forcefully than objective statements ever could. And the truth is that God is involved with his people intimately even before they are born.

Can the teaching of Psalm 139:13-16 be confirmed elsewhere in Scripture? Yes, it can. Virtually all the themes we have been reviewing concerning the unborn child—that God is actively involved in the development of the unborn, that life is a gift from God and a blessing, that God cares for the unborn and has a special purpose for them, that there is a continuity between life in utero and life after birth—may be found in these four verses. There is no good reason to call into question the message of this Psalm.

Our attention is immediately caught by the graphic way the child's development is described in verse 13: "Thou didst form my inward parts [literally: kidneys];/ Thou didst weave me in my mother's womb." The idea of weaving, as one commentator remarks, suggests the process whereby the basic frame of man is covered and laced by series after series of sinews, muscles, blood vessels, and tissues (cf. Job 10:11). By saying God *formed* and God *weaved*, the psalmist reveals that development is more than a clinical or biological happening; it concerns more than a woman and her doctor. God is at work in the process.

That life is a wonderful gift is stated in verse 14: "I will give thanks to Thee, for I am fearfully and wonderfully made." David realizes he is special before God and that thankfulness and reverence are due. This response of worship and praise is natural: "Wonderful are Thy works,/ And my soul knows it very well."

In verse 15, David recounts not only that he was made by God, but also that God showed intimate love and care in the process. David's frame was not hidden from God, though it was hidden from man. God was making it in secret. Long before the parents were ever aware of the process, God's special attention was fixed on David.

Verse 16 states further: "Thine eyes have seen my unformed substance." God's watchful and caring eye oversees what is taking place in the womb. Although the terms used here are to some degree figurative, there is still no way to discount the main truth of the passage that God has a profound love and concern for the unborn. If a person's worth is based on God's establishing a relationship with him, then surely the child in the womb qualifies.

The same verse further reveals that God has a purpose in mind for the unborn: "And in Thy book they were all written,/ The days that were ordained for me,/ When as yet there was not one of them." The last phrase suggests God's thoughts are focused on the child even in the earliest stages of fetal development, if not before.

Finally, the entire psalm underlines the continuity of prenatal and postnatal human life. As John Stott has explained:

> The psalmist surveys his life in four stages: past (v.1), present (vv. 2-6), future (vv. 7-12), and before birth (vv. 13-16), and in all four refers to himself as "I." He who is writing as a full-grown man has the same personal identity as the fetus in his mother's womb.[19]

We could also approach the psalm this way. David begins by speaking of the inescapable presence of God and of God's knowledge of everything about him (verses 1-12). God knows when David sits down and stands up, and even knows what David will say before he utters a word. God will not allow David to escape from his presence. Such truth, David says, is too difficult to grasp.

But why is God so intimately concerned about him? The answer is provided in verses 13-16: God is his maker, even in the womb! Before he knew God, God knew him. Before his eyes viewed the outside world, God saw him. Before his form became visible to the world, God marvelously formed him.

This is true of us all. But abortion is a denial of this truth. Abortion is a denial that God is involved in the development process; abortion is a denial that life is a blessing and gift; abortion is a denial that God cares for the unborn; abortion is a denial that God has a purpose for the unborn; abortion is a denial that the unborn child is a person.

The conclusion of the psalm is revealing. David speaks of how precious it is to know of God's special love for him (vv. 17-18). Then with just displeasure, David reacts strongly against the idea that there are men who shed innocent blood:

O that Thou wouldst slay the wicked, O God;
Depart from me, therefore, men of bloodshed.

David asks the Lord to reexamine his own heart and thoughts to see if there is any "hurtful way" in him of which he is unaware.

A reading of Psalm 139 can only evoke holy caution and respect for unborn life. In no way can we conclude that the fetus is nothing other than an object waiting to become human at birth or some later point. To use the term *fetus* or *parasite* in order to reduce the child to a *thing*, an *it*, that may be aborted cannot be justified from Scripture. The womb is holy ground, for God is at work there.

Scripture Is Clear!

We may have been prone to think Scripture could not answer the moral issues of our day. Yet God's Word is still sufficient to respond adequately even to the issue of abortion. We find that the entire ethos and underlying assumptions and themes of Scripture provide a thorough and clear response to abortion.

Who are persons with a right to life? All those in God's image. Are any people to be excluded? No, especially not the poor, children, handicapped, or elderly. *All* people are to be treated as persons with dignity and respect.

Is biological life a key clue to personhood? Clearly so, for a fundamental unity exists between body and soul. The Bible does not allow for a radical separation between those merely "biologically alive" and "persons."

Is death ever a good alternative? No, not even in the face of suffering. We should do all we can to eliminate suffering, but seeking death (for self or others) to escape suffering is not an option supported by Scripture.

When does human life begin? At conception. Does God bestow the value on unborn life that would indicate true personhood? We have every reason to believe this is so. The relationship God establishes with us at conception and throughout in

utero development is quite sufficient for establishing the personal value of the unborn. No Scripture supports abortion; on
the contrary, God is viewed as overseeing all of life from the
moment of conception.

> There can be no doubt that God clearly says the un-
> born child is already a human being, made in the
> image of God and deserving of protection under the
> law.[20]

It seems proper to conclude this chapter with reference to
the incarnation. Gabriel told Mary she would have a child, and
that conception by the Holy Spirit would mark the beginning of
the child's life. Most interpreters think Jesus' participation in
humanity began where every human life begins—at conception.
This observation is crucial, for it tells us that in God's sight,
human life at every stage of development is the object of God's
redeeming love. In this respect, Jesus' conception and life in the
womb of Mary provide a new and profound dignity for all unborn children.

Chapter 5, Notes

1. Genesis 4:1, 17; 21:2; 29:32, 33, 34, 35; 30:5, 19, 23; 38:3, 4.

2. Consider the prophetic curse on Ephraim: "As for Ephraim, their glory
will fly away like a bird—/No *birth*, no *pregnancy*, and no *conception*!"
(Hosea 9:11). Even used figuratively, the order is precise from conception on.
Also note Job 15:35; Psalm 7:14; Isaiah 33:11; 59:4, 13.

3. Bruce K. Waltke ("Reflections from the Old Testament on Abortion,"
Journal of the Evangelical Theological Society 19 [1976] :11) writes: "Now
these inspired writers and poets do not contest the fact that there is a causal
connection between sexual intercourse and conception; in fact, our advanced
knowledge about the DNA molecule and the genetic code fits comfortably into
the Biblical revelation, which has much to say about man's sexuality. But they
regard sexual intercourse as merely the means whereby God, the first cause of
all things, gives his blessing. Claudius Matthias expressed the Biblical view
well when he said, 'It went through our hands, but comes from God.' And
Luther gave expression to the faith of the saints when he said, 'I believe that
God created me.'"

4. God promised Abraham that his seed through Sarah would be as the
stars of the sky in multitude. This promise was most frustrating for Sarah, who
remained childless; she perceived that the Lord had "prevented" her from bearing children (Genesis 16:2). "Then the LORD took note of Sarah as He had
said, and the LORD did for Sarah as He had promised. So Sarah conceived and

bore a son to Abraham in his old age" (21:1-2). Rebekah was barren. Isaac prayed on her behalf, "and the LORD answered him and Rebekah his wife conceived" (25:21). In the case of Leah and Rachel, "Leah was unloved, and [God] opened her womb, but Rachel was barren" (29:31). Then after some time, "God remembered Rachel, and God gave heed to her and opened her womb. So she conceived and bore a son and said, 'God has taken away my reproach'" (30:22-23). Throughout the Genesis narrative, numerous references tell of God's giving or withholding conception.

5. Cp. Genesis 1:22; 8:17; 49:22.

6. Professor John Frame points out another argument regarding conception. The Bible is filled with references to the importance of sexual purity, that sexual intercourse is to be enjoyed within the bonds of marriage and that the marriage relationship mirrors the relationship between Christ and the church. Frame then asks, "If God is so jealous to maintain His lordship in this area of human life, is it conceivable that the product of sexual intercourse—the unborn child—should be wholly consigned to the whims of his parents?" (John Frame, "Abortion from a Biblical Perspective," *Thou Shalt Not Kill*, ed. Richard L. Ganz [New Rochelle: Arlington House, 1978], 46-47.)

7. Waltke, "Reflections," 12.

8. Psalm 51:6 reads: "Behold, Thou dost desire truth in the innermost being,/And in the hidden part Thou wilt make me know wisdom." Bruce Waltke holds that the Hebrew words for "innermost being" (*tehoth*) and "hidden part" (*satem*) refer not to David's innermost parts, but to his mother's womb. In this case, truth and wisdom are part of his former experience in utero. This interpretation of v. 6 is possible, due to its close relation to v.5 (Ibid., 13). Cf. John Jefferson Davis, *Abortion and the Christian: What Every Believer Should Know* (Philadelphia: Presbyterian and Reformed Publishing House, 1984), 41f.

9. George Eldon Ladd, *A Theology of the New Testament* (Grand Rapids: Wm. B. Eerdmans Publishing Co., 1974), 403.

10. Harold O. J. Brown, *Death Before Birth* (Nashville: Thomas Nelson Publishing House, 1977), 126.

11. Davis, *Abortion and the Christian*, 49.

12. Job 1:21; 3:11; 10:18; 31:15; Psalm 139:13-16; Jeremiah 20:17-18.

13. Frame, "Abortion," 50-51. Some scholars try to make reference to the passages in Jeremiah and Job where they mourn the day they were born and wish they had been spontaneously aborted (Job 3:3-10; Jeremiah 20:14-18). But neither Job nor Jeremiah thereby intended to teach that abortion is all right in certain circumstances.

14. After Bruce Waltke changed his position (see our discussion in chapter three) he wrote that he still considers the text to be referring to a miscarriage. But he says: "A more serious objection to the way in which I used the passage, however, is the illogical conclusion I drew from it. It does not necessarily follow that because the law did not apply the principle of *lex talionis*, that is "person for person," when the fetus was aborted through fighting that the fetus is less than a human being. The purpose of the decision recorded in this debated passage was not to define the nature of the fetus but to decide a just claim in the case of an induced abortion that may or may not have been accidental. If the miscarriage occurred accidentally, then it would have been regarded as manslaughter, a crime not necessarily punishable by death. However, in the

preceding case law the judgment did not apply the principle of *lex talionis* in the case of a debatable death of a servant at the hands of his master. But it does not follow that since "life for life" was not exacted here that the slave was less than a fully human life." See Waltke, "Reflections," 3, n.3.

A more recent pamphlet on this issue written by Ronald B. Allen (*Abortion: When Does Life Begin?* [Portland, Ore.: Multnomah Press, 1984], 9-14) points out in addition to Waltke's arguments that an accidental miscarriage such as we find in Exodus 21:22 is not the same thing as abortion-on-demand as presently practiced. Allen also maintains that the concept of a premature live birth is a "modern notion" and that a miscarriage is the most natural reading of the text. I would have to respectfully disagree. For children to be born prematurely is not a new thing, and the precise Hebrew words used in Exodus 21:22 seem to allow only for a birth and not a miscarriage. Allen is right, however, in noting that the dominant view historically has been that the passage refers to a miscarriage.

15. John Warwick Montgomery, "The Christian View of the Fetus," *Birth Control and the Christian*, ed. Spitzer and Saylor (Wheaton: Tyndale House, 1969), 87-89; J. W. Cottrell, "Abortion and the Mosaic Law," *Christianity Today*, 16 March 1973, 602-5; Frame, "Abortion," 50-57. See especially H. Wayne House, "Miscarriage or Premature Birth: Additional Thoughts on Exodus 21:22-25," *The Westminster Theological Journal* 41 (Fall 1978) :108-23.

16. Meredith G. Kline, "*Lex Talionis* and the Human Fetus, *Journal of the Evangelical Theological Society* 20 (September 1977) :194.

17. Ibid., 194ff. Professor Kline, after carefully analyzing both the words and the context, has proposed this view:

> [Verse 22] "envisages the death of a mother in giving birth pre-maturely to a live, uninjured child, and the law prescribes that the assailant must give for his forfeited life whatever the husband demands." [In verses 23-25,] "the law requires that if the child suffers calamitous injury or death the penalty payment must be a just equivalent." (p. 200)

In other words, when the men strike the woman in verse 22, she dies, but the child is still delivered. "No harm" therefore refers only to the child, not the mother. The penalty is monetary due to the fact that the mother's death was accidental, not intentional. Verse 23 refers to the possible death or serious injury to the child, in which case an exact form of justice must be carried out.

At first glance, this interpretation may seem somewhat farfetched. But upon further reflection it makes a lot of sense, or at least some version of it. Kline examines closely *all* the terms used in that law. The word for "strike" (*ngp*) is used elsewhere of "fatal divine judgments" and for "slaughter in battle." In fact, it is used in the same chapter in Exodus 21:35 for the fatal attack of a goring ox. So Kline suggests that the term for "strike" does not simply mean a push or shove, but probably refers to a fatal blow to the mother or child.

Kline agrees with the second interpretation that the clause, "so that the child departs" is best suited to a premature live birth. This would mean that while the mother received the fatal strike, the child was still able to be delivered. Kline points out that the verb for "fined" denotes punishment, which could be a fine but could also be punishment in general, including physical punishment. He then explains in depth how the punishment in verse 22 probably refers to the principle of ransoming a forfeited life, in this case the mother's. Thus, the penalty in verse 22 is a very serious one, similar in nature to Exodus 21:30, "If a ransom is demanded of him, then he shall give for the redemption of his life whatever is demanded of him."

In verse 23, "if there is any serious injury" refers to the child, either through miscarriage or other possible injuries. The penalty in this case is the *lex talionis* principle, which is a general statement requiring that strict justice be applied. It is designed for situations with a variety of possible injuries. It is not advocating a blind "life for life, eye for eye" kind of justice. The *lex talionis* statement, says Kline, has graphic terms "meant to express only the general principle that the offense must receive a just punishment. Relevant factors such as criminal negligence instead of intentional murder are taken into consideration. So the "life for life" formula does not preclude the application of the ransom principle seen in verse 22.

This may all seem a bit confusing, especially if one is not used to working with the Hebrew. But one conclusion is clear. The first interpretation of Exodus 21:22 referring to a miscarriage is not possible. Interpretations 2 and 3 are both possible, though this author tends to agree with Professor Kline. In either case, the value of the fetus is being stressed, not denied! Moreover, this passage is directed strictly toward accidental premature birth. But abortion is not accidental; it is the premeditated taking of the unborn human life.

18. John R. W. Stott, "Does Life Begin Before Birth?" *Christianity Today*, 5 September 1980, 50f.

19. Ibid.

20. Brown, *Death Before Birth*, 127.

Chapter 6

Barriers to Consensus

*T*hese scriptural arguments, I hope, can lead toward an evangelical consensus on the issue of abortion. But it seems one thing still blocks such agreement for many Christians: their hearts. They have a hard time wanting to hold a hard line against abortion when it comes to individual cases.

As one young woman said to me, "I believe abortion is wrong. But when a friend of mine thought her fifteen-year-old daughter was pregnant, I could feel my heart battling my head."

The hearts of many call out for freedom of choice. They find it easy to be sympathetic with the mother in distress. Justice for the unborn takes a second seat to pity for the mother.

Unwantedness: A Case Study

I recently read an article about a Christian woman who chose to have an abortion. The author, a close friend of the woman's, wrote the article to lend credence to the position that a woman should have the right to terminate an unwanted pregnancy.[1]

The author's friend was a professing Christian, thirty-eight years old with three children ages fourteen, eight, and six, who found herself with an unwanted pregnancy. She reasoned, "Just as people should not take away life carelessly, they should not give it carelessly. We don't want another baby." She reminisced about how happy she had been during her former pregnancies because she loved children and wanted to be a mother. But now she was tired of the prospect. It was just at the time in her marriage when her family could plan pleasant vacations together, and there were sufficient funds for music lessons and good colleges. She spoke of the "possibilities of life" for her present family; but, she argued, "we couldn't do those things with another baby."

Yet this mother was troubled by her decision. She confessed she had been upset when she asked her doctor about having an abortion. And there was a moment apparently, in her conversation with the author, when it was an effort for her not to cry. The agony of her decision appeared in such statements as:

> I don't think it is the right thing to do. But it's more right than to have an unwanted baby. . . . I can't convince myself that I don't owe my unborn baby anything, so I have worked something out with myself. The abortion will be on Tuesday. A week from today. So, every Tuesday for the rest of my life, I will do something special with my own three children or somebody else's child, in a conscious effort to add to life some of the possibilities I must take away. . . . Don't ever tell anyone I did this. I don't think they would understand.

How important it was that this woman receive proper guidance! Unfortunately, there is no hint in the article that she was pointed to Scripture, no mention of encouraging her to ask God for wisdom and strength in this difficult situation. Nothing, of course, was mentioned of the child already being two months alive and fully formed and growing. One worries about the guilt that is clearly evident in her tears, her desire that no one should know, and her attempt to compensate for the decision for abortion. A conflict was going on in her soul over the need to care for the child rather than to abort it.

Of course, we could critique the mother's reasoning as well as the author's counseling. But we are not in the mother's shoes. She is struggling between two possible responses: self-denial for the sake of the child or self-fulfillment for herself and her family. The author, consciously or otherwise, is setting compassion for the mother over against what is right for the child, freedom of choice over against the right to live.

COMPASSION FOR THE MOTHER VERSUS JUSTICE FOR THE CHILD

What Compassion Is Not

Those who support abortion are sensitive to the charge that they lack compassion and are unwilling to give themselves for their children, that they are cold and indifferent to life in the womb. Their only recourse is to claim compassion for the mother and to set that over against justice and the law.

The mother may be a teenager with her schooling and life's ambitions still before her, or a poor woman with too many children already. Perhaps she is in her forties and faces the increased possibility of complications for both herself and the child. We must try to put ourselves in the mother's shoes, they say—and of course we should.

We must also, they argue, have compassion on the child. Perhaps the child would be handicapped for life or end up in the degrading cycle of poverty. Sociologists suggest an unwanted child will likely suffer psychological damage. To these worries are added slogans such as, "Every child a wanted child," or "The most loving thing you can do for a child who is unwanted is to abort it."

But nothing is ever said about the rights of the child or that the child needs to be protected from assault. What is right or wrong is determined almost entirely by focusing on the mother's needs and burdens. We are reminded of our case study and the mother's statement defending her decision to abort: "I don't think it is the right thing to do. But it's more right than to have an unwanted baby."

Certainly, in the process of this debate, both compassion and "what is right" have become confused. Is it "more compassionate" or "more right" to take the life of a baby than to bring it into the world, though unwanted? (Actually, I am not at all convinced that in the case of this woman the child would have remained unwanted. The baby probably would have won over the hearts of the entire family even before birth.) As Christians, we should realize that God gave us his law for our benefit, not to make us unhappy. It is only when we deliberately reject God's law that we find ourselves in the agony this woman experienced.

Confusion is obvious in the slogan, "The most loving thing you can do to an unwanted child is to abort it." Love is equated here with destroying an unwanted child. Is love more compatible with the taking of another's life, or with the giving of one's life for another? Is it not true that the most loving thing you can do for an unwanted child is to want it, to care for and love it? If you say, "It is better to have an abortion than to bring an unwanted child into the world," for whom is it better? For the child, who will be eliminated through one of the gruesome techniques of abortion? Or for the mother, who may end up hating herself for it?

Why are only two alternatives presented, abortion or being unwanted? Cannot something be done about the problem of unwantedness? If the mother is unable to give love, what about the long waiting lists of people who wish to adopt? As many adoption agencies have been arguing, "There are no unwanted children, only misplaced ones."

It is inconceivable that if a child is unwanted because it is a burden or inconvenience, one simply gets rid of the child. Imagine a husband saying he no longer wants his wife. Does that mean she is of no value and is better off dead? Perhaps you would counsel him to get rid of his wife—"It is the most loving thing you can do for her." Killing her would eliminate the problem of unwantedness.

In a superb paperback entitled *Who Broke The Baby?*, Jean Garton points out that to say a child is unwanted tells us nothing about the child. When parents say, "She is precious," or even

"He is naughty," they are describing the child. But when they say, "He is unwanted," they are not describing the child; they are describing themselves. It is not the child who is deficient but the parents. The unwanted child is not the victim of his own shortcomings but that of his parents.[2]

Compassion and Justice

What all these examples serve to illustrate is that compassion cannot be set over against justice. In Scripture these two virtues are united in the very character of God who is both loving and just. As Psalm 89:14 assumes:

> Righteousness and justice are the foundation of Thy throne;
> Lovingkindness and truth go before Thee.

The Old Testament stresses God's love for the weak and oppressed and at the same time his justice against the oppressor.

In Jesus—God manifested in the flesh—love was an outstanding feature. His love extended not only to his family and friends but even to his enemies (Matthew 5:43-48). Jesus taught that the two greatest commandments were to love God with all your being and to love your neighbor as yourself. These two commandments serve as the foundation for all the law of God. It is important for Christians to realize, over against Joseph Fletcher and situation ethics, that love is in harmony with the law of God. Love does not contradict "You shall not murder." As John wrote, if you love God, keep his commandments (1 John 5:3).

Because love and justice have characterized God's dealings with mankind, Christian personal and social ethics have maintained that love and justice should likewise govern our relationships to one another. As Micah declared:

> And what does the LORD require of you
> But to *do justice*, to *love kindness*,
> And to walk humbly with your God
>
> (6:8).

In a similar way, Jesus accused the religious leaders of Judaism:

> For you tithe mint and dill and cummin, and have neglected the weightier provisions of the law: *justice* and *mercy* and faithfulness; but these are the things you should have done without neglecting the others" (Matthew 23:23).

Both justice and love are essential requirements in Christian ethics. Doing what love demands is the same thing as doing what God commands (1 John 5:2), not in a legalistic way as a list of rules to be followed, but in a humble way, knowing that God is love and has our own best interests at heart. Not only does the Bible tell us to love one another, but it tells us quite precisely *how* to love one another. Consider, for example, Ephesians 5:1-3:

> Therefore be imitators of God, as beloved children; and walk in love, just as Christ also loved you, and gave Himself up for us, an offering and a sacrifice to God as a fragrant aroma.
>
> But do not let immorality or any impurity or greed even be named among you, as is proper among saints; . . .

This is the only passage in Scripture where we are told directly to be "imitators of God." Notice that such imitation is contrasted with acts of impurity and greed.

What Is Compassion?

We return then to ask, What does one do with an unwanted child? This is the crucial question. It has a larger dimension and can be asked of many categories of people. What do you do with the poor who drain tax dollars, the handicapped who demand our time and energy as well as our money, the hungry and diseased masses of the world who need food and medical aid? How do you treat the odd, peculiar, or unlikable?

Historically, we have seen society resort to two ends of the spectrum in its response toward the unwanted. On the one side has been the cruel response of the world—that of fear and dislike, even hatred—that seeks to eliminate others in order to protect one's own interests. The idea is to control the environment so as not to be hurt by others, and thereby have maximum enjoyment of one's own life. In the past, mankind has seen fit to kill, to abandon infants, to allow starvation, to go to war, as well as to abort, in order to achieve this enjoyment and security. Nazi Germany is a clear example of this.

On the other side is the example of Christ. To the leper who was banished by society and untouchable by law, he did not say, "It would have been better if you had not been born." Instead, he stretched out his hand and touched him and said, "I am willing; be cleansed" (Mark 1:41). To the children rejected by his disciples, he held out his arms. To the sinners and tax-collectors despised by many, he offered fellowship and forgiveness. For the hated Roman soldiers who crucified him, he asked his father to forgive them.

In the place of fear and hatred was profound love. Rather than insulating himself from the leper's disease or a poor man's need or a strong man's aggressiveness or a sinner's unrighteousness, Jesus gave himself to them all, regardless of the consequences. His primary motive was not to keep himself from suffering or inconvenience. Rather, he sought to remedy situations through the selfless giving of himself. In Jesus Christ we understand clearly the meaning of love (*agape*), a sacrificial giving to one another.

We ask, "What would Jesus do with an unwanted child?" Would he eliminate the child or love and protect it? Mother Teresa spoke like Jesus when she responded:

> I am very grateful to receive [the Nobel Peace Prize] in the name of the hungry, the naked, the homeless; of the crippled, of the blind, of the lepers, of all those people who feel unwanted, unloved, uncared [for] throughout society; people who have become a burden to society and are shunned by everyone.[3]

How does compassion work? It begins by receiving compassion. "We know love by this, that He laid down His life for us; and we ought to lay down our lives for the brethren" (1 John 3:16). Having our own needs met by Christ, we then cultivate a sensitivity toward the needs of others and commit our resources to meet their needs. We act instinctively as Christians, not stopping to count the cost. We do not ask whether the person is deserving of our love. We simply respond as Christ would respond.

This is why it is so disconcerting to see Christians reacting to social issues from the world's perspective. Ironically, the primary indictment brought against the evangelical church by its contemporary critics is its failure to display compassion toward the unwanted and dispossessed of society. While there are the John Perkinses and Sojourners of our movement, we generally insulate ourselves from confrontation with human need.

There was a time when the church's witness was effective because of its demonstration of selfless compassion toward the needy (Acts 4:32-35):

> And the congregation of those who believed were of one heart and soul; and not one of them claimed that anything belonging to him was his own; but all things were common property to them. *And with great power the apostles were giving witness to the resurrection of the Lord Jesus, and abundant grace was upon them all.* For there was not a needy person among them, for all who were owners of land or houses would sell them and bring the proceeds of the sales, and lay them at the apostles' feet; and they would be distributed to each, as any had need.

Sandwiched between references to caring for the poor is the record of their powerful witness to the resurrection of Christ. The apostolic church was simply applying the commandment, "You shall love your neighbor as yourself." This law of compassion had been written in their hearts and found expression as the Holy Spirit directed them to give out of their abundance, thus fulfilling Old Testament laws such as we find in Deuteronomy 15:1-11.

But the church today has lost its effective witness in the world. What if the evangelical church took a major stand to help the poor, and sacrificed and inconvenienced itself for the weak and helpless? Would not God then bless such righteous suffering for the furtherance of his kingdom? Our course could be redirected by the way we respond to the human needs surrounding abortion.

Curtis Young of the Christian Action Council, in his very practical book, *The Least of These*, explains how churches can become involved. He focuses first on the spiritual ministry of the church—counseling women who have had abortions, leading them to the forgiveness Christ alone can provide, praying for them, showing Christ's boundless love. Then Young focuses on possible outreach ministries of the church—providing shepherding homes for pregnant women who find themselves alone and rejected, and developing Crisis Pregnancy Centers to help women with crisis pregnancies. Young reasons, "Since we urge women to carry their babies to term, we must be prepared to minister to them after the babies are born."[4]

Prolife groups such as the Christian Action Council in Washington, D.C. have sought consistently to provide guidance for compassionate responses to abortion. The problem has been the lack of interested persons and financial support. Nevertheless, the present growth of Crisis Pregnancy Centers throughout America is nothing less than phenomenal. This is what compassion is about—reaching out in a sacrificial way to both mother and child.

One Crisis Pregnancy Center received this letter from a girl:

> My abortion is something I wish I had never done. I can remember looking at the doctor when it was done and saw him putting my baby in a plastic bag and then, throwing it away in a garbage bag. Do you know how that feels? . . . Have you ever lost something you

loved dearly? I did, and I'm not proud of it. . . . If I had a place to go and people who cared about my baby and me, maybe my baby would be born and alive. . . . You people are against abortion, but are you willing to help young girls and women who don't have the money or a place to live? . . . Some of us women and girls are not killers. We're human too. And I can tell you having an abortion is killing me slowly.

Another girl wrote:

Rev. Young, I wish that I had found one of your centers when I became pregnant over a year ago. Since then I have welcomed Christ into my life and I rejoice in this love and forgiveness! I want to help women choose life, avoid the pain and grief I have experienced, and rejoice in the love of Christ, our Lord and Savior!

The church must be ready to extend practical help both to unmarried women who are pregnant and to married women who find it difficult to cope with a pregnancy. The unmarried woman may especially need help—a place to stay or financial aid. She may need medical help or tips on how to care for her child. If she works, she needs to be assured that her child will receive proper care during her working hours. Her child may need exposure to a father figure. She will no doubt need spiritual counseling.

Francis Schaeffer, in *Whatever Happened to the Human Race*, remarks:

Christians and others who wish to see an end to inhumanities, in compassion and love must offer alternative solutions to the problems. . . . Merely to say . . . "You must not have an abortion"—without being ready to involve ourselves in the problem—is another way of being inhuman.[5]

What about the "Hard Cases?"

We still have those particularly sensitive circumstances during pregnancy that seem to defy a solution: when the life of the mother is in jeopardy, when the unborn is handicapped, and when conception results from rape or incest. Would not compassion for the mother in these circumstances necessitate abortion? And should we not insist in any future law that these be included as exceptions?

These hard cases have historically been the means of opening the door to abortion-on-demand. They are the main arguments of prochoicers defending abortion and the major reason why a consensus among Christians is elusive. What is the answer? In my opinion, it is not abortion.

Life of the mother. The life of the mother should not be pitted against the life of the unborn child. The lives of both mother and child are precious in God's sight. Compassion would lead a doctor to try to save both lives. In situations prior to viability when a pregnancy-related condition precludes the child's survival within the womb, such as with an ectopic pregnancy, the choice facing the doctor is to save the mother or to lose both mother and child. But that action is not the same as the deliberate taking of an unborn child's life because it is unwanted.

While saying that abortion is justified to save the life of the mother, many do not consider the fact that the vast majority of abortions-on-demand are done under this "therapeutic" umbrella. In fact, the reason stated on medical forms for over 95 percent of all abortions is "therapeutic." Yet less than 5 percent of all abortions are done for any of the so-called hard cases— saving the life of the mother, the prior knowledge of a handicapped baby, or conception resulting from rape or incest.[6]

Abortion-on-demand has been made possible today due to the broad way society has defined *therapeutic*. In the Supreme Court ruling of 1973, not only did the court rule that the unborn are not "persons in the whole sense," it also ruled that abortions could be performed even in the third trimester "where it is necessary, in appropriate medical judgment, for the preservation of the *life* and *health* of the mother."[7] These two exceptions—life or health—may sound narrow, but the court went on to define health as "all factors—physical, emotional, psychological, familial, and the woman's age—relevant to the well-being of the patient. All these factors may relate to health."[8]

In declaring this, the Court placed the abortion decision squarely on the shoulders of the attending physician: since "the abortion decision in all its aspects is inherently, and primarily, a medical decision, a basic responsibility for it must rest with the physician."[9] It also provided a loophole for abortion-on-demand throughout all nine months of pregnancy. Since all pregnancies have some consequences for a woman's emotional and family situation, no pregnancy is ruled out as a candidate for abortion.

One final point. Induced abortion to save the life of the mother is becoming rare due to the fine art of medicine. Two circumstances that still require it are the tubal pregnancy and the cancerous uterus. Since such pregnancies will only result in death for both mother and child, abortion has always been allowed for these and similar circumstances. No exception clause is needed under law.[10]

Those supporting abortion for therapeutic reasons should study more recent reports confirming that abortion can be damaging both mentally and physically, even in the hard cases of rape and incest.[11] Not to take these facts into account is indefensible today, especially since therapeutic abortion has become the loophole for abortion-on-demand.

Knowledge of a handicapped child in utero. Prior to the advent of ultrasound technology, amniocentesis was the primary source of knowing whether a fetus in utero was handicapped. But learning that the fetus was handicapped could not be put to positive use in helping the fetus until the third trimester of pregnancy. Thus, whenever amniocentesis was done in the second trimester, the only reason was to discover the handicap early enough to abort the child.[12]

There are two kinds of individuals affected by the birth of a handicapped child: the child with the handicap and those caring for him. Some think the child is better off dead, and they call him a nonperson. But Christians recall Jesus' love for the handicapped as persons of worth. God's solution to their problems was never to eliminate them or tell them they should not have been born. Jesus himself explained that the man born blind was born that way "in order that the works of God might be displayed in him" (John 9:3). God reminded Moses: "Who makes [man] dumb or deaf, or seeing or blind? Is it not I, the LORD?" (Exodus 4:11). God's solution has always been to love and care for the handicapped, and to encourage them to realize the dignity that is already theirs as those made in God's image.[13]

Parents are also affected by the birth of a handicapped child. They naturally react with great sadness over the handicap. Their aspirations for the child are suddenly forgotten. Many even find it difficult to cope with the presence of a handicapped child. But is abortion God's answer? Are we not to love as Christ loved? Should not the church share the burdens of these parents and help them take care of their child?

C. Everett Koop, who has treated many handicapped children in his thirty years as pediatric surgeon, reminds us of the desire of deformed children to live and of the unexpected blessings and joy such children often bring.[14]

There is always the temptation to think of handicapped persons with some prejudice. As Christians, we must bend over backwards to help the handicapped and their parents and be more sensitive to their needs and aspirations.

Rape and incest. Rape and incest are horrible experiences. But it is particularly difficult to counsel a woman who has experienced such trauma and is now pregnant. Still, there are compelling reasons for rejecting abortion as a solution to her anguish.

The main principle is: One wrong is not corrected by another wrong. One act of violence is not solved by another violent act. This is true for a number of reasons.

Abortion is a violent act. Its methods are physically violent, the painful effects on the child can be termed none other than violent, and the consequent effect on those participating in the abortion bespeaks violence, as we will see in the final chapter. The immediate and long-term effects of abortion on mothers is harmful both physically and psychologically.[15]

Physically, abortion is a major health risk. This is especially true of teenagers, and the younger they are, the higher the complication rate. Due to the abortion, women can develop incompetent cervixes, infections, or other complications that will keep them from ever bearing children again.[16] No one can predict these physical complications.

Psychologically, studies show that abortion can be equally damaging. Little evidence can be found to support abortion as psychologically therapeutic, whereas much evidence shows it can be harmful. How else does one account for the rapid rise of an organization such as Women Exploited By Abortion (WEBA)? In the first ten months of its existence, this organization grew from two members to ten thousand members who had previously had abortions but now are strongly prolife. It appears women instinctively view abortion as infanticide. Mental conflict from contributing to a child's destruction can be more detrimental than the duress of carrying a child to term.

Nancyjo Mann, founder and president of WEBA, summarizes what she has found to be the psychological effects of abortion:

> One psychological effect we see almost all the time is guilt. Others are suicidal impulses, a sense of loss, of unfulfillment. Mourning, regret and remorse. Withdrawal, loss of confidence in decision-making capabilities. They feel that maybe they've made a wrong decision, maybe they can't make another decision right in their life. Lowering of self-esteem. Preoccupation with death. Hostilities, self-destructive behavior, anger and rage. You can lose your temper quickly. A despair, helplessness, desire to remember the death date which is really weird but you do that. You remember these dates very strongly. A preoccupation with the would-be due date or due

month. My daughter was due in early March, so in early March it's there. . . . [17]

Clearly, abortion is not the psychologically therapeutic answer to the trauma of rape or incest.

Moreover, abortion for rape makes bad law for several reasons. First, to execute the child when the attacker is not given the death penalty is not right. The child, no less innocent or in need of our support than its mother, is also precious life.

Also, pregnancy resulting from rape is extremely rare. Approximately .06 of 1 percent of all abortions are for rape victims. Reasons for the lack of conception after rape include: emotional trauma preventing ovulation, impotence on the part of the attacker, use of contraceptives by the women involved, and so forth. Moreover, it takes time to conceive. If a woman receives immediate treatment with estrogen, conception can be prevented. In a Minnesota hospital, thirty-five hundred rape victims were treated, and there were no pregnancies. In Buffalo, New York, not one pregnancy has resulted from rape in thirty years. In Washington, D.C., a study of over three hundred rape victims showed only one resulted in pregnancy. [18]

To establish a law based on such an infrequent exception allows for misuse of that law. Hence the proverb, "Hard cases make bad law." Also, to enforce the law, legal proof that a rape has occurred would be needed, but such proof would take too much time. So, in practice, the mere claim of rape becomes the deciding factor for an abortion.

One final thought is important. Is the child of rape indeed an actual person? Consider the value of an Ethel Waters. Her mother was a twelve-year-old victim of rape by a white boy. The family considered abortion but rejected it. Ethel's life was a very difficult one, especially in childhood. But she was used by God in a special way, singing to hundreds of thousands in the Billy Graham crusades. Someone might argue that for every happy ending, several tragic stories of rape could be told. But the point is not whether everyone ends up happy. The question is whether the unborn are persons of value, even when they result from rape.

Abortion will never be anything but a destructive solution to a problem even as awful as rape and incest. If the intent is to help the injured woman, there are better ways to help than to destroy the child, which may only bring further emotional and psychological shock. If a victim of rape or incest asks in her distress for an abortion, friends tend to do what she asks. But what the woman in this situation needs is love and acceptance, not an easy fix. The more compassionate solution is to counsel her, show love and care, find psychiatric help if needed, and support her through delivery and beyond.

FREEDOM OF CHOICE VERSUS THE RIGHT TO LIVE

"Freedom of choice" is another slogan of those seeking to justify abortion, and one that compassionate Christians hesitate to oppose. It stands over against the "Right to life" slogan of prolifers. The two sides have become polarized as a result.

The thought that freedom to abort might be restricted or even taken away drives some proabortion advocates into a frenzy, and they make wild statements meant to suggest that the prolife movement is repressive. Feminist Lynn Walker makes the accusation: "The pro-lifers are dangerous people. They are not pro-children. They are anti-sex. And when they are done with women's rights, next come the Jews." Fay Waddleton, president of Planned Parenthood, adds: "The fundamental principles of individual privacy are under the most serious assault since the days of McCarthyism."[19]

On the other hand, we may find a devoted Christian saying with conviction: "I am personally opposed to abortion. It is repugnant to me. But I must support the right of others to choose abortion since we live in a free country. I cannot impose my moral convictions on others."

There are those who believe with sincerity that the ability to choose is what is important. If you have conscientiously struggled and wrestled with your choice on a matter, then the result should not be criticized.

There is also the matter of *privacy*. Government is encroaching more and more on the rights of individuals. Telephones are being tapped. More power is being given to the courts to intervene in the affairs of families. Many fear that the regulation of abortion could lead into regulation of other areas of life. Privacy must be protected against government.

Freedom is a popular notion. Everyone wants to be free. This quest for individual freedom has been a major force in changing values in society. "Getting out from under" has been modern man's obsession, and this kind of freedom always seems to involve a rejection of authority. But does freedom have no boundaries?

On one occasion when I was participating in a panel on abortion, a message was secretly attached to my table. It read:

What the world needs:
1. More fun;
2. More sex;
3. More contraception;
4. More sex education;
5. More wanted babies;
6. Fewer abortions (but because of 3, 4, 5);
7. Fewer moral bigots telling women how to run their lives;
8. Fewer mouths to feed;
9. And a lot of other things you folks find offensive;
10. You to leave us alone.

This message was written by someone who believed in freedom without boundaries. You can see by items 7 and 10 that the writer operates on the principle of autonomy (self-law); man is a law unto himself. Mankind determines ethical norms, and whatever norms are present are relative to man who creates them. There are no absolute norms, so individuals should be given the "freedom to choose" their own moral standards.

Freedom to Choose

The quest for freedom is a noble and virtuous activity. But freedom is not determined in a moral vacuum. In the abortion context, the slogan "freedom of choice" has become a euphemism for feticide.

That this is so is evident in several proabortion statements. Consider the slogan, "I wouldn't have an abortion myself, but I support the right of others to do so." This sounds broad-minded at first. But would it be broadminded to say: "I would not shoot at passing cars, but I support the right of others to do so"? Or as Julie Loesch, a prolife feminist in the antinuclear movement, says:

> It would never occur to us to say, "For private moral reasons I don't personally condone nuclear arms, but I can't really impose my feelings on my fellow citizens who don't hold the same religious beliefs—and certainly each nation has the right to choose to incinerate its enemies if it wishes."[20]

According to Dick Gregory and others in the civil rights movement, the "abortion as a matter of private morality" argument uses the same premise on which slavery was built. Protesting the treatment of slaves on a plantation was an invasion of privacy; slaves belonged to their owners.

The owner of an abortion clinic in Jackson, Mississippi, has said, "No one has the right to make a decision to prevent another person from making a decision about abortion, or any other subject."[21] But what would happen if this were the case?

Clearly, the *object* of the choice is all important. Society cannot grant "freedom of choice" where fundamental principles of justice are involved, whether those principles touch on life and death matters or on secondary concerns such as paying income taxes. It would be ludicrous to claim that "no one has the right to make a decision to prevent another person from committing murder or robbery or rape." Yet this is precisely what the abortion clinic owner would have us believe. Freedom of choice can never justify freedom to take innocent human lives. Those who clamor for freedom of choice, adamant in their insistence that the choice rests solely with the mother and her doctor, studiously avoid the point that abortion kills a human being.

A similar argument goes like this: "It does not matter what you eventually choose; the fact you have struggled and wrestled with your choice is what counts." To hold this position, one must also argue that there is no absolute right or wrong.

In other contexts, we accept that one person's freedom cannot infringe on the freedom of others. Logically, the right to life comes before the rights to liberty and the pursuit of happiness. Without it, force and strength decide everything. A stronger person's convenience takes precedence over the life of the weak. For freedom to mean anything, the right to exist must be maintained. It underlies and sustains every other right we have.

One reason we have laws is to protect the weak from the strong. When those laws no longer exist, violence becomes inevitable. This is what has happened since 1973 with abortions; the laws protecting the unborn were nullified, and millions of abortions have occurred since.

We must be careful not to confuse the oppressor with the oppressed. Freedom to abort becomes an oppressive claim over another person's life. There is no greater measure of oppression than the claim of one person to decide whether or not another shall be given the right to live. According to Harold O. J. Brown, "freedom of choice" in the abortion context "has all the boldness and simplicity of a totalitarian final solution."[22]

Brown also points out that the "right to life" is a natural right based on natural law, without which one cannot live. On the other hand, "freedom of choice" is a derived right based on positivistic law. One can live without making choices, but one cannot make choices without being alive! Common sense dictates that the right to life is a precondition to the enjoyment of freedom of choice, the necessary foundation upon which all other human rights are built.

It is argued, "A woman has a right to control her own body." But does this right allow a woman to infringe on the rights of others? Women who are seeking freedom and equality

cannot achieve it by denying freedom and equality to the unborn. To do so is to deny the very principles on which their own
quest for freedom and equality stands.[23]

Yes, women have been denied equality in many ways—un-
equal pay, sexual harassment, problems in job promotion. Because of these inequalities, many within the feminist movement
have viewed freedom to abort as necessary in order to maintain
control in their drive for equality. They view children as burdens
that hinder women from keeping pace with men. Some people
have an obsession to control their own lives, and some will even
destroy anything they cannot control. This, I think, is what is
happening in abortion.

But who is in control of whom? Those having abortions
often seem to be women whose lives are out of control. They are
unable or unwilling to assume the consequences of their prior
actions. After all, an unborn child does not cause a woman to
become pregnant. Parents acquire an obligation to any child
they conceive, and they have no right to kill the child in order to
terminate that obligation. As Mary Drumm, vice president of
the Council on Adoptable Children, put it:

> Unfortunately, after a woman is pregnant, she cannot
> choose whether or not she wishes to become a
> mother. She already is, and since the child is already
> present in her womb, all that is left to her to decide is
> whether she will deliver her baby dead or alive.[24]

Responsible living includes control of oneself prior to the
"need" for an abortion. Sexual activity is not a foregone conclusion for the unmarried. The cycle is morally bankrupt—sex outside marriage causes children to be conceived toward whom no
obligation is felt.

When it comes to moral values, our nation has lost its way.
Someone has compared the present attitudes toward sex with
that of past generations. For the Puritans, sex included both responsibility and pleasure. For the Victorians, sex was responsibility without pleasure. Today in America, sex is pleasure without responsibility. Shelly Douglass writes in *Sojourners*:

The question of abortion, I think, begins with the question of responsible sexuality. Our culture has moved from a horror of sexual intercourse as something gross and degrading, an evil mitigated only by its purpose of procreation, to a demand for free sexuality exercised for the pleasure of it and without any connection with childbearing. I believe that both extremes are oppressive to persons, especially to women.[25]

We must begin talking about the myth of control. Many prolife feminists argue that women are deceiving themselves if they think they are controlling their lives through abortions. Rather, they are sacrificing their womanhood to fit into a society built for men. For, sadly, the rules of society are not structured for the equality of men and women. Pregnant women, or women who value their family ties, *do* find the unspoken rules of society against them. Should a woman then respond to this injustice by trying to deny her womanhood? Daphne DeJong refers to the women's movement presently as "processing women through abortion mills to manufacture instant imitation-men who will fit into a society made by and for wombless people."[26]

A lack of respect for women and a lack of shared responsibility, men with women, for the care of children are some basic reasons why women resort to the destruction of life in the womb. This is why the family structure is so important in society, and why the church should not be ashamed to support it and promote what God had in the beginning ordained: "For this cause a man shall leave his father and his mother, and shall cleave to his wife; and they shall become one flesh" (Genesis 2:24).

The Myth of Choice

A young Christian friend of mine in a suburb of Chicago was surprised to learn of the high percentage of women initially seeking abortions whose views could be changed by further information. Counselors at a crisis pregnancy center and "sidewalk counselors" talking to women outside an abortion clinic near her home convinced a surprising number of women to carry the "unwanted" children to term.

"I'd always thought women having abortions had made a firm choice about it and knew what they were doing," my friend told me. "I didn't think there was anything that could be done to stop them. Now I see that many of these women really have not made a firm choice. They *don't* know what they are getting into with an abortion. And a lot of them deep down really *want* to do the right thing and keep the child. All they need is a little support against the pressure to abort it."

We have all heard that abortion is necessary as an option for freedom of choice—but we may also speak of the "myth of choice." Abortion undeniably involves both physical and emotional pain. Consequently, a woman will not choose the pain of abortion unless certain other negative factors are pushing her in that direction—parental or social pressure, personal problems, lack of funds, lack of support from a husband or a boyfriend, and so on. As Elizabeth Moore, head of Feminists for Life, has noted: "It is more likely in fact that women submit to abortions, not so much because they have the choice, but because they feel that in their own circumstances they have no choice at all."[27]

This feeling of entrapment is often true of the poor. Whereas the poor are often more person-oriented than the rich and have been more prone to question the morality of abortion, nevertheless more and more poor people are finding their way to abortion clinics. Because the poor lack the basic necessities of life such as adequate food, housing, and jobs, government social services have been able to lure them into the elimination of their unborn. Their poverty seems to negate their right to make choices. Of course, there is an alternative for the poor. Were Christians to help them get on their feet, the poor would see no need for such abortions.[28]

But we do not have to go to the poor to find women under pressure. Society is such today that subtle pressures for abortion come from many directions. Consider this woman's story:

When I was twenty-one I became pregnant. I was un-married, a university student and I supported myself by working at night. . . . I fit your description of a woman who should qualify for an abortion exactly. Very busy and very poor. However, I did not want to have an abortion on moral and dare I say it . . . religious grounds. I believe abortion is murder. . . . My belief is heartfelt and therefore when I became pregnant, although I was completely ambivalent about my condition I could not seek abortion as an escape route.

The first doctor I went to assumed I wanted an abortion before I said anything to him and I had to tell him very firmly that I did not need his "help."

The Planned Parenthood worker who first diagnosed my condition was incredulous at my decision and in a manner bordering on hostility said to me, "Didn't you always secretly want to have a child so that you could have someone to love?" Sitting there, literally shaking with terror at the disastrous news, I was sub-jected to the amateur psychology of a pro-abortion advocate who simply could not believe that my reluc-tance to have an abortion was based on private scruples. And that was the beginning of a very long and painful trial by fire. I lost my friends because they could not "tolerate my stupidity.". . .

At one point I was offered a large sum of money so I could go to New York and get it done "quietly." I had pictures of the vacuum machine used for abortion shoved in my face, and a detailed account of the whole procedure outlined for me, until I cried. Every time I sat down in the student pub someone would start: "Why don't you have an abortion?" and later, "Why didn't you?". . . I caused anger, too, I believe, because my refusal to have an abortion was based on moral and religious grounds. My answer was not an excuse, it was a judgment, and it was probably seen as a judgment on all those who disagreed with me. . . .

Now older and married . . . I often sit and wonder about the future of women like me who say no. I think about the fact that I was twenty-one, and telling everyone to go to h— was infinitely easier for me than it must be for a very young teenager, who, although she feels the truth of her unwanted fetus' humanity in her soul before she ever feels the first life movement in her belly, must face outraged parents, social workers who have seen too many tragedies to care anymore, and terrified boyfriends. Authority figures can be overwhelming when you're only fifteen. I wonder, and my heart reaches out with compassion to every woman who has had an abortion against her wishes. True, nobody can legally drag you on the operating table, but they can certainly use social and financial cattle prods to get you there.[29]

What strikes one upon reading this account is the way society pressured this young woman to have an abortion. They tried, but she was strong enough to resist. As Mary Meehan observes: "Freedom of choice is a mockery when so many teenagers are pressured by their parents, and older women by husbands or boyfriends to avoid children they want to bear and raise."[30] I often wonder how many Christian parents have pressured their daughters to get an abortion in order to "cover up" their daughters' sin.

Numerous illustrations may be cited, but we will only review one more. It concerns a high school junior who was forced by her parents into having an abortion. This girl's story appeared in a *Washington Post* article published in December 1980. While a young girl can get an abortion without her parents' consent, there was no means for stopping these parents from forcing their daughter into having an abortion.

According to the reporter, the girl wanted to have the baby. "Her desire may have been prompted by rebelliousness, or perhaps a teenager's abbreviated vision of the future, or love for the father. Whatever the moral, cultural and ethical forces gathered within her, she went and declared that she would 'not murder [her] baby!'" But the inevitable pressures came. The family doctor tried to convince her that legally she was not carrying a life. Her mother insisted it would be madness for her to become a "child-mother." Finally, her mother drove her to the clinic where she was forced to have the abortion.

The outcome in this case was quite sad. Emotionally, the young woman remained in a state of depression. Her hostility reached a peak when in desperation she called her mother a "murderer." She confided in a friend, "They made me kill my baby." Physically, she continued to experience some pain and discomfort. Then at 2:00 A.M. one morning, her parents were awakened by a scream. She was experiencing shooting pains. Rushed to the hospital, the doctors decided to operate and found "products of conception" that had been left in the uterus as well as some infectious fluid.

In spite of this tragic affair, the reporter still believed the girl's abortion was necessary and that we must preserve "freedom of choice" for abortion. What freedom of choice was there? The doctor in his impressive office with all his learning telling a young woman only one side of the story, or the mother demanding that her daughter was not going to be a "child-mother"? These examples serve to show us that to a great extent, freedom of choice is a myth.

Moreover, by their words and actions, the leaders of the prochoice movement have shown they are not really for choice. Often we are met with statements such as this one by abortion rights activist Dr. Jane Hodgsen:

> We have laws regulating limits on marriage, driving a car, drinking, voting—we even try to regulate movie viewing according to age. But motherhood knows no limit. Is adolescent pregnancy a disease?

We have laws regarding other epidemics such as— we have mandatory immunization, but we have no law prohibiting motherhood before the age of 14 in our supposedly-civilized society. . . . Shouldn't we, instead of merely asking for freedom of choice for these patients, shouldn't we at least *demand* that they have an equal financial and moral support through government funding for the youngster who opts for abortion? Shouldn't we even go a step further and *mandate* against continuing pregnancy in the very young—say those less than 14 years? How can there be freedom of choice when the adolescent is so often uninformed, misinformed, unable to grasp the consequences and is being pressured into motherhood?[31] (italics mine)

At the same conference where Hodgsen was speaking, another longtime abortion activist, Dr. Lonny Myers, stated:

I will not support the right of a 14-year-old to have a baby. I don't believe that women have the right to reproduce indefinitely. I will not stand up and say they have the right to have ten or twelve children when you have no means of support, when you have them and deposit them on society.[32]

In brief, what these abortion advocates are arguing is that young teenagers and certain other mothers should have no freedom of choice.

Another obvious fact is that those *for* freedom of choice are also *against* informed consent legislation. Informed consent bills in state legislatures seek to provide safeguards whereby women would not be herded into abortion mills. Every woman seeking an abortion would have to be informed of the possible problems inherent in the operation and of the present state of the fetus. For a *real choice* to take place, all pertinent information must be presented. But Planned Parenthood and other prochoice organizations have consistently lobbied against such legislation.

What a misguided direction! These "prochoice" advocates are clearly pressing toward a society in which abortion is a common occurrence but without a clear, informed choice.

In the final analysis, then, to support the "freedom to choose" in the abortion context is to support permissive abortion. There are not three positions from which to choose—antiabortion, proabortion, and freedom of choice—there are only two: prolife and proabortion. For freedom of choice is a cover for upholding the freedom to have an abortion, the basis for abortion-on-demand today, and it denies the freedom of the child to choose life.[33]

The Biblical Definition of Freedom

Why do prochoice arguments not make sense to most of us? We have a different view of freedom. We know that freedom does not come through a mere lifting of restraints.

Scripture presents freedom as a gift from God. In the Old Testament, God graciously delivered Israel out of slavery in Egypt. This gift of freedom was not without restraints; it was not some kind of license for libertinism that comes with human autonomy. Israel's freedom remained bound to the Giver, and desertion of Yahweh resulted in the loss of that freedom.

A circular pattern developed in Israel during the period of the judges. Whenever Israel sinned against God, he would allow the nation to be oppressed by another. Once Israel repented, God graciously delivered them from their enemies and gave them *freedom*. For Israel, freedom was a gift from God, but a gift that demanded righteous living. Whenever they followed the Lord, he blessed them with freedom. Whenever they reverted to sinful autonomy, God gave them over to the oppression of their enemies.

The New Testament develops this concept of freedom in its deeper dimension. Jesus said, "If you abide in My word, then you are truly disciples of Mine; and you shall know the truth, and the truth shall make you free." Conversely, he said, "Truly, truly, I say to you, everyone who commits sin is the slave of sin. . . . If therefore the Son shall make you free, you shall be free indeed" (John 8:31-32, 34, 36).

Ultimately, one is either a slave of sin and the devil, or a slave of righteousness and of God. If we are slaves to sin, then deliverance is a gift from the Son whereby God's forgiveness and salvation are ours, and we are effectively made subject to God's will.

Clearly, Scripture sees all mankind as basically not free, unable to live autonomously. The man who is truly free is free only to live righteously in loving service to God and fellow man. That is what man is designed for. Author Susan Schaeffer Macaulay says that man's seeking freedom to escape this design is like a fish seeking freedom by leaping out of the water and into a boat. Is he free? No, his casting off of "restraint" has led to his own destruction.

The world interprets freedom as no interference, no restraints. When God dares to place restraints on my freedom, he becomes my enemy. Of course, this has happened historically. God put restraints on Adam and Eve, and they rebelled. Ever since, mankind has been at enmity with God, rebelling against his restraints. God's restraints are meant for our good and our freedom, but we rebel against them; and the wages of such sin is death. Like fish out of water, this kind of freedom can only lead to our destruction.

The irony is that God, the only one free from external restraints, came down into all this struggle against restraints in order to release those in bondage to sin. Jesus humbled himself *under* the restraints that we might be free to worship and serve God. In the words of Paul:

> But when the fulness of the time came, God sent forth His Son, born of a woman, born under the Law, in order that He might redeem those who were under the Law, that we might receive the adoption as sons (Galatians 4:4-5).

What a contrast this is with those who wish to be free from all rules so that they may take away another's right to live.

We arrive then at an unforeseen conclusion. Of the two sides, the prolife movement is really the side promoting true freedom. They are fighting for the most defenseless of God's creatures. By defending the innocently inconvenient, the unwanted unborn, they are more properly promoting the cause of freedom. For they are putting the right to live and freedom from assault above personal and selfish interests.

Not long ago I stood at the side of the hospital bed of a little girl who was dying from cancer. Her mother was forced to stand by and watch her little girl cry in pain, slowly dying. Two days later, my wife and I returned with a stuffed animal, only to find that the little girl had died minutes earlier. It was all very heartbreaking: a little child dying, in pain, while her mother and the doctors struggled to save her.

But today across America, 1.5 million to 2 million mothers per year are deliberately taking the lives of their little ones, causing their own babies excruciating pain in the process, all in the name of *freedom*. Even the medical profession, once sworn to alleviate pain and to cherish the unloved, has those within its ranks who have become enemies and adversaries of the unborn. Only the prolife movement stands between these little ones and death.

Chapter 6, Notes
___

1. Ina J. Hughes, "I'm Not My Mother and I Do Have a Choice," *Presbyterian Survey*, January 1981, 51.

2. Jean Staker Garton, *Who Broke the Baby?* (Minneapolis: Bethany House Publishers, 1979), 30. Garton further notes, slogans that state that the most loving thing you can do for an unwanted child is to abort him sound compassionate and loving, but in truth they hide "self-gratification and self-indulgence," and convey a false sentimentality that condones destruction as an expression of love. Society says, I will love this child *if* he is convenient or has perfect form or *if* he is compatible with my plans. Society is "attempting to solve its social, economic and personal problems by the sacrificial offering of its children" (pp. 26-34).

3. An excerpt from an unofficial transcript of Mother Teresa's remarks on accepting the 1979 Nobel Peace Prize in Oslo.

4. Curt Young, *The Least of These: What Everyone Should Know About Abortion* (Chicago: Moody Press, 1983), 177-78. For his entire discussion, see pages 161-79.

5. Francis A. Schaeffer and C. Everett Koop, *Whatever Happened to the Human Race?* (Old Tappan, N.J.: Fleming H. Revell Co., 1979), 113. For the entire discussion, see pages 113-18. Helpful articles on understanding some of the deeper problems involved in helping pregnant women who are poor may be found in *Christianity Today*, 20 May 1983, 14ff.

6. This is a conservative estimate. The closest estimate is probably more like 3 percent.

7. *Roe* v. *Wade*, 410 U.S. 113 (1973), p. 165.

8. *Doe* v. *Bolton*, 410 U.S. 179 (1973), p. 192.

9. *Roe* v. *Wade*, 410 U.S. 113 (1973), p. 166.

10. That induced abortion to save the life of the mother is rare may be evidenced by a statement of Dr. Alan F. Guttmacher who was president of Planned Parenthood World Population and the one who moved Planned Parenthood into the abortion field. In 1967, Guttmacher wrote: "Today it is possible for almost any patient to be brought through pregnancy alive, unless she suffers from a fatal illness such as cancer or leukemia, and if so, abortion would be unlikely to prolong, much less save life" ("Abortion— Yesterday, Today and Tomorrow," in *The Case for Legalized Abortion Now* [Berkeley, Calif.: Diablo Press, 1967]). With the advent of modern medicine, the true "therapeutic" abortion has become virtually extinct. It is no longer a proper treatment for disease; instead, it has become the rationale for abortion-on-demand.

11. See our discussion in chapter 6 on rape and incest and in chapter 7 on emotional trauma and suicide.

12. Strange but true, the March of Dimes has been a leading proponent and funding source for programs of amniocentesis. The March of Dimes representatives insist they are simply trying to help parents anticipate children with birth defects. But reports in medical journals show the high percentages of handicapped babies which, when detected, are aborted. In one report (*New England Journal of Medicine*, 25 January 1979), over 3,000 women were tested with amniocentesis. Of these, 113 handicapped children were detected, of which 105 were aborted, including 2 normal babies. In another report (*OB-GYN News*, 1 October 1975), 62 handicapped babies were detected of which 60 were aborted and the remaining 2 were lost in miscarriage.

13. For our discussion of the handicapped, see chapter 4 and the section, "Can Anyone Be Excluded from Personhood?"

14. Schaeffer and Koop, *Human Race?*, 63ff.

15. For a series of articles dealing very carefully with both physical and psychological complications following abortions, see the volume *New Perspectives on Human Abortion*, ed. Thomas W. Hilgers, Dennis J. Horan, and David Mall (Frederick, Md.: University Publications of America, Inc., 1981), 69-163. We are also especially indebted to the extensive research prepared by The National Committee for a Human Life Amendment, Inc., for "Arguments in support of Hyde Amendment (Section 209) to the 1980 Labor-HEW Appropriations Bill," pp. F1-20. Possible medical complications from abortions include: hemorrhage/blood transfusions, torn cervix, perforated uterus, strombosis/lung blood clots, fever/peritonitis, infection, sterility, premature births,

miscarriages, tubal pregnancy, and low birth weight in future pregnancies. Some of the most common psychological reactions following abortion include: discomfort with children, feeling victimized, feelings of low self-worth, guilt, anger, depression, grief, regret, loss, preoccupation with aborted child, frequent crying, and suicidal tendencies.

16. "Legalized Abortion and Public Health," *Institute of Medicine: National Academy of Sciences*, May 1975, 62.

17. Nancyjo Mann, "Women Form WEBA to Fight Abortions," *The Washington Times*, 3 August 1983.

18. "Zero Pregnancies in 3500 Rapes," *The Educator*, September 1970; B. M. Sims, "A District Attorney Looks at Abortion," *Child and Family*, Spring 1969, 176-80; David Granfield, *The Abortion Decision* (New York: Doubleday and Co.), 107-8.

19. Statements are quoted in a syndicated column by Joseph Sobran, "Will the Real Yahoos Please Stand Up?" *Jackson Daily News*, 13 April 1981.

20. Julie Loesch, as quoted by Mary Meehan, "The Other Right-to-Lifers," *Commonweal*, 18 January 1980, 14.

21. An article entitled "Pro-choice at New Woman Medical Center," *Jackson Daily News*, 11 October 1980, quoting Martha Fuqua, owner of the clinic.

22. Harold O. J. Brown, "The First Amendment and the Question of Justice in Light of the Abortion Issue," *New Perspectives on Human Abortion*, 298-99. According to Dr. Gordon Zahn ("Abortion and the Corruption of Mind," *New Perspectives on Human Abortion*, 338): "One suspects that slogans advocating freedom of choice are a rhetorical ploy designed to balance slogans advocating right to life on the other side of the issue. But in one very important sense they are not equivalent. The protection of human life is generally taken to be an unequivocally approved objective, so much so that it is usually considered the *raison d'etre* for society itself. Freedom of choice, on the other hand, is a value which, while no less approved, is recognized as being subject to limitations arising from society's obligations to protect and defend human life. One is not free to kill the employer whose decision to dispense with an employee's services will worsen the already strained financial resources upon which that employee's family depends. No one is free to destroy something (or someone) simply to avoid a passing inconvenience."

23. According to Elizabeth Moore (as quoted in *National Right to Life News*, May 1980, 3), head of Feminists for Life in Washington D.C., "The basic value upon which just law must rest is not choice but equality." She believes that the "woman's right to control her own body theme" is a right wing argument that puts property rights above the right to life.

24. Mary O'Brien Drumm, "Meeting in the Radical Middle," *Sojourners*, November 1980, 23.

25. Shelley Douglass, "Without Judgment," *Sojourners*, November 1980, 18.

26. Daphne DeJong, as quoted by Mary Meehan, "The Other Right-to-Lifers," *Commonweal*, 18 January 1980, 15.

27. Elizabeth Moore, "A Matter of Welfare," *Sojourners*, November 1980, 16.

28. Ibid. Moore's entire article clarifies well the issue of abortion and the poor.

29. "One Woman's Story," *Pro-Life News/Canada*, April 1978, reprinted from a letter in the Lakehead University (Thunder Bay, Ontario) paper *Argus*, 3 February 1978.

30. Mary Meehan, "Will Somebody Please Be Consistent," *Sojourners*, November 1980, 14.

31. "'Pro-choicer' Asks: Should We Mandate Abortion for the Young?" *Minnesota Citizens Concerned for Life Newsletter*, June 1980.

32. Ibid.

33. In 1973, the Supreme Court found that a constitutional right to privacy took precedence over the right to life of the unborn. That ruling, which has led to millions of abortions, is the basis for the present day abortion-on-demand, and no amount of special pleading on the part of those defending "freedom of choice" can decree otherwise. We must view the slogan as a rhetorical ploy designed to offset the importance of slogans advocating the right to life.

Chapter 7

Have We Missed Something?

S ometimes as we discuss an issue, we may talk all about its ramifications but ignore the reality of what is taking place. This often is true of abortion: we talk of the moral and ethical issues surrounding it but not of the act itself. Abortion is not an easy, painless choice like cutting a fingernail or removing a wart. It is a killing—a violent killing.

Some do not know—or do not care—that abortion involves violence. Some Christians oppose other types of violence in society but deal with abortion by denying that the victims are human. They persuade themselves that violence in this one area will not spill over into other areas. Their arguments are not convincing on either account.

That the unborn are human beings is clear in light of our previous discussions and examinations of the biblical record. That there is violence in abortion and that this violence does indeed spill into other areas of society is the point of what follows. While this is not a pleasant subject, we must face the truth that abortion is the violent taking of a human life in the womb. As in other subjects of a gruesome nature, Christians dare not turn away from this issue. As the writer of Proverbs has written:

> Deliver those who are being taken away to death,
> And those who are staggering to slaughter, O hold
>   them back.
> If you say, "See, we did not know this,"
> Does He not consider it who weighs the hearts?
> And does He not know it who keeps your soul?
> And will He not render to man according to his
>   work?
>
>   (24:11-12).

Everything about abortion suggests violence: the methods used, the effects on those involved, the twisted language, and the violence spilling into other areas of life.

Violent Methods

The methods of abortion are physically violent. Whether it be a sharp, double-edged curette (or knife) by which the child is unceremoniously dissected, or the suction of the inserted tube which tears apart the tiny child, or the burning effect of the injected saline solution on the tender skin of the child while simultaneously poisoning the baby internally—there is no term more appropriate for such cruel methods than *violence*.

In dilation and extraction (D and E) abortions, a method being used more and more frequently against babies twelve to eighteen weeks after conception, fully formed and able to experience pain, the unborn are literally pulled apart as they are dragged out of the womb:

> Instead of a loop-shaped knife, a *grasping forceps* (similar to a pliers with teeth) is inserted into the womb to grasp part of the fetus. Because the developing baby already has calcified bones, the parts must be twisted and torn away. This process is repeated until the body is totally dismembered and removed. Sometimes the head is too large and must be crushed in order to remove it. Bleeding is profuse.[1]

It is not difficult to see how violent and painful this death must be for the child. Ironically, you couldn't do such things to a dog or a hamster. Laws regulate the killing of livestock and stray cats and dogs. But no laws regulate the process of aborting babies.

What appears quite evident is that babies in utero experience the pain of those abortions, though abortionists try to deny this. But just as we can observe a baby in utero recoiling from the prick of a pin when experiments in the womb are monitored, so the baby feels the cutting edge of the knife or the tearing apart of the suction device. In a very real sense, abortion is the most extreme form of child abuse.[2]

Most everyone has seen or heard about the new ultrasound film showing an actual abortion. The victim was an eleven-week-old fetus, a little girl—fully formed, even down to her fingerprints. It was a suction abortion, and the abortionist filmed it out of curiosity.

At the beginning of the film, the child can be seen playing, turning around, sucking her thumb; her heart was beating at the normal rate of 120. When the instrument touched the uterine wall, the baby immediately recoiled, and the heart rate rose considerably. The fetus had not yet been touched, but she knew something was happening.

Then the suction began. The child was literally drawn apart piece by piece; and while this was happening, the child was thrashing around, trying to escape the inevitable. Her head was thrown back and her mouth was open wide in what one doctor called her "silent scream." Her heart rate was over 200, and you could see the tiny heart beating rapidly. Finally, the forceps came in and crushed the head in order to remove it. The whole process took twelve to fifteen minutes.

When the abortionist saw the ultrasound, he left the clinic and never returned! This is a barbaric and painful way to die.

It is interesting to realize that ultrasound technology has been in place since 1976, and abortions have been going on far longer than that. Abortionists in California do their late D and E abortions using ultrasound as a guide for locating the unborn child and dismembering it.

Why, then, had no one made a tape of the procedure prior

to 1984? The answer is obvious. Those who defend abortion, in league with those who practice it and profit from it, must maintain a visual blackout to keep American women ignorant of the inexpressible cruelty embodied in the act of abortion. Not many women could view such a film and then voluntarily submit themselves and their children to such a procedure.

One further example of violence in abortion is informative. Around 16,500 fetal corpses were discovered in a large storage container outside a now defunct medical laboratory. While many of the fetuses were quite small, some weighed as much as four pounds and were estimated to be in the sixth month of development or older. The bodies were preserved in formaldehyde-filled jars which in turn were stacked in cardboard containers.

News photographers who came to the scene were not permitted to take pictures. Photographs were later obtained from a Los Angeles pathologist who had been asked to examine the babies' bodies for possible legal action. Forty-two vivid slides of mangled, aborted fetuses—some torn apart by D and E abortions, some with crushed skulls, some burned and poisoned by the salt procedure—were shown. *Washington Post* columnist George Will then made this pertinent comment:

> Most pro-abortion persons have a deeply felt understandable need to keep the discussion of abortion as abstract as possible. They become bitter when opponents use photographs to document early fetal development. The sight of something that looks so much like a child complicates the task of trying to believe that there is nothing there but "potential" life. And if fetal pain is acknowledged, America has a problem. Its easy conscience about 1.6 million abortions a year depends on the supposition that such pain is impossible.[3]

It is alarming to note that all saline abortions take place during the second trimester of pregnancy (months four through six) when the baby is fully formed. We wince at the prospect of nuclear war and the burning devastation it would cause for the living. Yet, with a salt abortion, the burned skin of the child, when delivered, resembles skin soaked in acid. In fact, it may take up to two or three hours to kill the child this way while he struggles against the pain.

Violent Effects

Violence is also reflected in the psychological and spiritual effects on those involved in performing abortions. Abortion brutalizes not only the mothers but also the medical personnel performing them. To cope with the procedure, a part of reality must be blocked out. But society is learning more and more of abortion's negative psychological effects.

Those for abortion like to accent the psychological trauma for women who are compelled to keep their children. But which is more psychologically harmful, keeping or aborting one's child? We have already called attention to Women Exploited by Abortion (WEBA), whose phenomenal growth has been due to the negative psychological effects of abortion.[4]

There are cases of depression among women so severe that they have led to suicide. A surprise witness before a Cincinnati City Council in 1981 was the regional director for Suicides Anonymous. Speaking in support of a parental notification ordinance for minors seeking abortion, she stated:

> Suicide is assuming frightening proportions. In the U.S.A. in 1978 there was one attempt every 16 minutes. Today there is one attempt every minute. Adult suicide is up 400%, teenage suicide 500%. In 1978 there were 60,000 successful suicides. . . . This Cincinnati group has seen 5,620 members in 35 months. Over 4,000 were women *of whom 1,800 or more had had abortions.* The highest suicide rate is in the 15 to 24 age group. There is a direct linkage between suicide attempts and [abortion]. It is an act of cruelty to remove parental duties and rights during the abortion crisis.[5]

To appreciate these figures, we must understand that suicide among pregnant women is rare, only one-fourth that of the general female population. Moreover, prior to legalization, a fifteen-year study in Minnesota revealed that suicide rates for women were only 25 percent those of men. Now, however, since the legalization of abortion, not only have suicide rates for women surpassed those of men, but we see figures such as those presented in Cincinnati.

Psychiatrist-obstetrician Judith Fogel, a doctor who does abortions, has said:

> I think every woman . . . has a trauma at destroying a pregnancy . . . she is destroying herself . . . a psychological price is paid . . . it may be alienation, it may be a pushing away from human warmth, perhaps a hardening of the maternal instinct. Something happens on the deepest levels of a woman's consciousness when she destroys a pregnancy. I know that as a psychiatrist.[6]

A psychological study reports that at the conscious level, women who have had abortions often show only a relatively mild degree of anxiety and depression. But at a much deeper, unconscious level, abortion is regarded by many women as infanticide. Deep-seated guilt, remorse, and sadness set in. Instinctively, they realize they have taken the life of their child.[7]

Some academicians and counselors wish to bypass these realities by saying the guilt of these women is exaggerated; it should not really be there. The fetus is only "potential life." But the truth is that such grief and sorrow cannot be reduced so easily. The guilt can be overpowering. Have you ever felt that God could never accept you because of something you had done? It is a profound guilt. And if we minimize what the woman has done, we rob her of the opportuniy to bring her guilt before the Lord Jesus and to know and experience his cleansing and forgiving power.

Someone has said, "It is easy to scrape a baby out of the womb, but not so easy to scrape the aborted baby out of the mind." Barbara Hammond of the Christian Action Council received this letter from a girl who had an abortion:

> People that have never experienced being pregnant and having an abortion would never know how much pain girls like us go through. It really hurts. The night I got back from Planned Parenthood, I called my best friend and was crying. I told her that I wanted my baby back. I saw the doctor throw my baby in a trash can. And that tore me up. Now I think that my baby is piled under all kinds of trash.
>
> I wish now that I never had my abortion. My family and friends tell me to put the past behind me. Forget about it—but I can't. There is always that scar in my heart that my baby is dead. It hurts like h—. . . . It can tear a person in half.[8]

In this same letter, this young girl wrote the following poem about her child:

> One day, Baby, we'll be united in a world where no
>   one can divide us
> So don't you worry, Baby, I'll be along soon.
> I didn't mean to do the thing I did to you.
> So please forgive me, and always remember you're
>   in my heart forever and ever.
> This time nobody will rob you from your life,
>   because I'll be there to protect you forever.

A mother who compelled her daughter to abort her child many years ago tells of how she still cries each time she thinks about it: "No one knows of the torment that can come after it is over, unless they have gone through it. We could not talk about it for years, and still it is hard. . . . This is my first grandchild!" This grandmother was under a physician's care for two years due to emotional stress.[9]

These same feelings are experienced by the fathers as well. Dr. Arthur Shostak of Drexel University in Philadelphia revealed that 72 percent of the men he interviewed in a four-year study disagreed with the statement that "males generally have an easy time of [abortion] and have few, if any, lingering disturbing doubts." Since this type of research is so rare, he requested funding for further research from the National Institutes of Health. "They told me off the record that this type of work could be construed as anti-abortion," he said. "It could indicate that the absence of counseling is leaving behind *a destructive residual* in many men. It would be seized upon by anti-abortionists." So they denied his request. [10]

It is common knowledge that one of the greatest problems generated by abortion is its negative effect on physicians and staff. Some of the most staunch prolife supporters, such as Bernard Nathanson, were at one time abortionists. [11] Two main speakers within the prolife movement in Jackson, Mississippi, are women who used to perform abortions. One, Dr. Beverly Smith McMillan, opened the first abortion clinic in Jackson. Following a life-changing experience in which she accepted Christ as her Lord and Savior, Dr. McMillan realized what she was doing was wrong, and resigned. She confesses: "The good news that makes the Gospel so relevant today is that God forgives. I know from personal experience that the blood of Jesus can cover the sin of abortion." [12]

Another woman, a nurse practitioner, helped perform abortions in a clinic for two and a half years. She did this for economic reasons, having three children to feed and no child support. Finally, she and another nurse resigned. (The drop-out rate is especially high among nurses.) This nurse told of a young neighbor girl who had just had an abortion and had cut her wrists in attempted suicide. It is foolish to suppose that abortion does not have grave aftereffects on both the women and the practitioners.

A report presented at the 1977 annual meeting of the Association of Planned Parenthood Physicians describes the negative psychological reactions doctors may have after performing D and E abortions. The report began by explaining that in the past, women applying for second trimester abortions were psychologically vulnerable, since prostaglandins were used (or saline) and the women went through the trauma of labor and delivery of a dead fetus.

Now doctors are changing to D and E abortions using general anesthesia. But this has shifted the emotional problems from the patient (and the nurse attending the patient) to the doctors. The report reads:

> When performing a D&E abortion, the gynecologist is aware of being the active agent in the procedure. On the one hand, the doctor is sparing the patient the pain and emotional distress of the amnio abortion. On the other hand, he or she is the one who is crushing and dismembering the fetus in a D&E procedure, which can be emotionally disturbing. . . . As the doctor tends to take responsibility and assume guilt for the procedure, she or he may have disturbing and recurrent ruminations or dreams. Doctors have found that these negative reactions decrease as they get used to the procedure, decrease if fewer D&Es are done per session, and may depend on their feelings about the woman's reason for needing a late abortion. . . . Because of these problems, it is important that participation in D&E abortions be entirely voluntary, and that doctors have a chance to talk over their feelings with understanding colleagues or counselors.[13]

Apparently, while the D and E may be better emotionally for the woman, it is having a very negative effect on the physicians.

Violent Language

Another form of violence is psychological: the use of demeaning or deceptive language to cover up the destruction of human lives. Language can distort a person's worth. If someone can be dehumanized through the rhetoric used to describe him, a major victory over him has been won. By distorting the image of enemies or victims, one can justify what he wants to do to them and not feel he did anything wrong.

It happened in the nineteenth century when slaves were considered nonhuman or subhuman. They were mentioned in the category of livestock: men were the drivers, women were the breeders, and children were the increase. In Nazi Germany, the Jews were called nonhuman . . . a huge mass . . . parasites.

Language can also distort violent actions. From Vietnam, reports came back of the "attrition of unfriendly forces" and the "tactical reduction of M.V.A. cadre." This referred to the number of enemy dead. "Body count" referred to our own dead, "selective ordnance" to the use of napalm, "pacification" and "protective-reaction strikes" to bombing raids. Such semantic cover-up is usually employed when trying to defend the indefensible. Euphemisms are used when the reality is too ugly. By inventing a special language, society can name things without calling up mental pictures of them. "Pacification" does not sound much like killing; neither does "termination of pregnancy."

When a child is wanted, the doctor calls her a baby. When she is unwanted, the doctor may call her a fetus, a product of conception, or any of a number of cover-up terms. What has changed is not the child itself but the terms used to describe the child. Doctors may speak of abortion as "heading off delivery" or the "interruption of pregnancy." Abortion clinics use euphemistic names such as Planned Parenthood or Women's Reproductive Health Center. Those pushing euthanasia speak of "mercy killing" and "death with dignity." We need to remember what the Bible says about this:

> The words of the wicked lie in wait for blood,
> But the mouth of the upright will deliver them
> (Proverbs 12:6).

Yes, there is a language of violence. The evidence is overwhelming that language is often used to distort truth and deceive. But while language can blind us to what is happening, pictures have a way of delivering us from this blindness.

During the sixties, many were upset when the television networks showed pictures of Vietnamese children burned by napalm. They called it "bleeding-heart propaganda." But the nation's eyes were opened. Visitors to Dachau in Germany or Yad VaShem in Jerusalem are struck by the pictures of horror of the holocaust. Likewise, pictures of aborted children, or pieces of aborted children, have had their effect. They represent not just "emotional propaganda" but what is truly happening. They tell the story accurately. The pictures and graphic details are not what make abortion look ugly and brutal. Abortion itself is ugly, brutal, violent, and uncivilized.

Again, we may turn to an appropriate proverb:

There are six things which the LORD hates,
Yes, seven which are an abomination to Him:
Haughty eyes, a lying tongue,
And hands that shed innocent blood,
A heart that devises wicked plans,
Feet that run rapidly to evil,
A false witness who utters lies,
And one who spreads strife among brothers
(Proverbs 6:16-19).

Violence Spreads
The relation between abortion and other forms of violence is clearly suggested by the correlation between abortion and child abuse statistics. Government statistics reveal that since 1970, an annual increase of 18 to 20 percent in child abuse cases has been reported. The argument before the Supreme Court in 1973 was that "unwanted children" become child abuse statistics. Yet during that same period, unwanted children were decreasing at a rate of over one million annually. According to Dr. Westhoff of the Center for Disease Control, "the United States is approaching the point at which all of its legitimate babies will be wanted at birth by their parents."[14] All wanted babies, yet

epidemic child abuse! These statistics, not coincidentally, correlate with those of other countries that have adopted permissive abortion laws.

Dr. Phillip G. Ney, in a symposium at Loyola University, estimated that if the 18 to 20 percent annual rise in battered children since the seventies continues, the decade of the eighties will witness 1,500,000 battered children, with 50,000 deaths and 300,000 permanent injuries. His research indicates:

> Abortion decreases an individual's instinctual restraint against occasional rage felt toward dependents while simultaneously diminishing the social taboo against attacking the defenseless. An aborting society devalues unborn children, hence also diminishes the value of born children. Persons who abort also increase their guilt and self-hatred, which may be taken out on other children. The mothering capacity of a mother for future children is also diminished by previous abortions.[15]

A clear example of this was a woman who killed her three-year-old son just one day after obtaining an abortion. Because she was under "the influence of extreme mental and emotional disturbance," according to the testimony of a psychiatrist, the jury recommended imprisonment instead of the death penalty.[16]

We have seen a vast increase in violence in our society during the past two decades. The fact that violence is not limited to confrontations between strangers but reaches into the home is a matter of deep concern. We read not only of battered children but of battered spouses, battered parents, the abuse of the elderly and handicapped. Ponder too the corresponding increase of abortions worldwide—there are now 60 to 75 million abortions annually—and we can understand the principle stated so well by Mother Teresa: "If a mother can take the child in her womb, what is it for me to take you or for you to take me?"[17]

The prolife movement is for nonviolence. It holds to the principle that abortion will never be anything but a violent and destructive solution to a social or personal problem.

Bless the Beasts and Children

As Christians, we need to be aware of society's ambivalence toward the value of innocent human life. At times, life can be treated with respect, at other times with disdain. Consider the March of Dimes. This philanthropic organization is known for doing a great deal of good for handicapped children. Yet, at the same time, it supports and funds genetic tests on the unborn during the second trimester of pregnancy.[18] Because such young babies in utero cannot be treated medically, these tests are clearly for the purpose of detecting handicapped infants in order to abort them. The March of Dimes argues that by identifying "normals," they save some from abortion. But conversely, when a handicapped child is found, the March of Dimes washes its hands of the situation and says it is up to the parents to choose.

A little more than a decade ago, the musical duo The Carpenters released the song, "Bless the Beasts and the Children," title song to a film of the same name. The song pleads for the rights of these two oft-victimized groups:

> Bless the beasts and the children,
> For in this world they have no voice,
> They have no choice.

In our country, many individuals and groups do try to stand up for the rights of the "beasts." Abigail Van Buren, author of the "Dear Abby" column, was asked if she sided with a dog named Sido who was condemned in the will of an elderly woman to be "kindly" put to death when she died. Abby responded:

> I am for preserving Sido's life. This is another example clearly showing that *what is legal is not always moral*. And if the law gives an animal owner the right to destroy a healthy pet, then the law should be changed.[19]
>
> (italics mine)

Strangely, Ms. Van Buren is a strong supporter of legalized abortion.

The Massachusetts Supreme Court ruled by a 6 to 1 margin that a man could not award goldfish as prizes in games of chance. It reasoned that such practices "dull the humanitarian feeling" of prize winners.[20] The same court made Medicaid funding of abortions mandatory throughout the state.

A direct mail appeal stated its philosophy this way: "Life must be saved by non-violent confrontations. . . . Our ethic is not only to personally bear witness to atrocities against life; it is to take direct action to prevent them."[21] This was not an appeal from a right to life organization; it came from Greenpeace, a group trying to "save the whales." The letter pleads with us to "help end this atrocious slaughter." They rely on "people who believe . . . in the irrefutable right of whales to live, in harmony, with other forms of life."

I mention these examples not because I am unconcerned about whales or other animals—Christians should seek to respect and preserve God's creation—but because there is a certain irony in the fact that society, mainly through the Supreme Court decisions, has erected obstacles against the protection of unborn *human* life. We have better medical care than ever before, yet legalized abortion now claims around two million children every year—children who are dumped in garbage bins or flushed down disposals all across the United States.

In the midst of all this violence, we should ponder the proverb that reads:

> He who justifies the wicked, and he who condemns
>   the righteous,
> Both of them alike are an abomination to the LORD
>   (Proverbs 17:15).

Or again,

> There is a way which seems right to a man,
> But its end is the way of death
>   (Proverbs 16:25).

Chapter 7, Notes

1. This description of a D and E was given to the author by a doctor who formerly did abortions. Another description of a D and E was given in a paper presented at the Annual Meeting of the Association of Planned Parenthood Physicians in Atlanta, Georgia, 13-14 October 1977. The paper, entitled "Second Trimester Abortion by Dilation and Extraction (D&E): Surgical Techniques and Psychological Reactions," written by Drs. Sadja Goldsmith, Nancy B. Kaltreider, and Alan J. Margolis, read in part: "When the amniotic fluid had drained, the placenta and fetus were removed; the fetus was extracted in small pieces to minimize cervical trauma. The fetal head was often the most difficult object to crush and remove because of its size and contour. The operator kept track of each portion of the fetal skeleton in order to be sure of complete evacuation. Finally, a blunt or sharp curette and a 12 mm vacuum aspirator were used, which often yielded additional tissue fragments. The patient was then transferred to the recovery room, watched for about two hours, and sent home with a friend" (pp. 2-3).

2. Concerning the pain of the unborn, see John T. Noonan, "The Experience of Pain by the Unborn," *New Perspectives on Human Abortion*," 205ff.

3. George Will, "Abortion Painful for the Aborted," *The Washington Post*, 5 November 1981.

4. See our discussion in chapter 5.

5. "Alarming Testimony Given in Council," *Right To Life of Greater Cincinnati, Inc. Newsletter*, September-October 1981.

6. Judith Fogel, *Los Angeles Times*, 7 March 1971.

7. Dr. Ian Kent, *Psychiatric News*, 3 March 1978.

8. For this and similar examples, contact the Christian Action Council, 701 West Broad Street, Suite 405, Falls Church, VA 22046.

9. Ibid.

10. James McBride, "Men and the Pain of Abortion: A Close-Up," *National Right to Life News*, 22 February 1982, 5.

11. Cf. Bernard N. Nathanson, *Aborting America* (Garden City, N.Y.: Doubleday, 1979).

12. Dr. Beverly A. McMillan, "I Changed My Mind About Abortion," *Good News: The Bimonthly Magazine for United Methodists*, March-April 1984, 13.

13. Goldsmith, Kaltreider, and Margolis, "Second Trimester Abortion," 6.

14. Dr. Charles F. Westhoff, "The Decline of Unplanned Births in the United States," *New York Times*, 3 January 1976. Statistics confirm that child abuse has risen dramatically in countries with permissive abortion laws. In Great Britain, child abuse increased tenfold; in Japan, where abortion has been freely practiced for over twenty years, infanticide has become so frequent it is now a major national concern. Clearly, unwanted pregnancies are not the reason for child abuse, but abortion itself appears to contribute to the problem.

15. Dr. Phillip G. Ney, Symposiums on the Psychological Aspects of Abortion, Stritch School of Medicine of Loyola University, October 31-November 1, 1975.

16. "Woman Kills Three-Year-Old," *National Right to Life News*, 13 October 1983, 12.

17. An excerpt from an unofficial transcript of Mother Teresa's remarks on accepting the 1979 Nobel Peace Prize in Oslo.

18. The March of Dimes Birth Defects Foundation issues a number of pamphlets explaining their position, for example, "Genetic Counseling" (1983) or "Facts—1985." They say their position on abortion is one of "neutrality." However, numerous articles in the *National Right to Life News* have shown a distinct bias of the March of Dimes against the unborn handicapped. See for example Anthony Ventura, " 'Adolescent Pregnancy' Program Illuminates NRLC Difficulties with the March of Dimes," *National Right to Life News*, 22 April 1982, 6; or John Cavanaugh-O'Keefe, "March of Dimes Promotes Amniocentesis," *National Right to Life News*, 7 September 1981, 3.

19. "Dear Abby Backs Right to Life—for Animals," *Minnesota Citizens Concerned for Life Newsletter*, July-August 1980.

20. "Court Votes Pro-fish," *National Right to Life News*, 28 September 1981.

21. " 'Atrocious Slaughter' Must Be Halted," *Minnesota Citizens Concerned for Life Newsletter*, November 1981.

Conclusion:
Toward an Evangelical Consensus

During the past two decades, opposing viewpoints on abortion have been carefully analyzed. Scripture has been studied in detail, and the issues are in clearer focus now than ever. The logical premises of abortion-on-demand have been uncovered.

As a result, the evangelical community is awakening to the fact that abortion is a violent and destructive solution to social or personal problems. Due to the enormity of that violence (some eighteen million abortions within only thirteen years, or enough to wipe out the present populations of North Carolina, South Carolina, Georgia, Alabama, Mississippi, and Tennessee combined), abortion has become an issue for action, not compromise.

Some evangelicals believe that, due to our fallenness, life's decisions have become morally ambiguous and extremely complex, especially as applied to the medical sciences. Therefore, one must take a middle-of-the-road position. A simplistic or absolutistic view (i.e., totally prolife) is the easy way out.

I disagree. Standing firmly for life is not an easy answer. To argue that the issues are too difficult and complex to make a decision is the easy and simplistic solution of the middle ground. It is always easier to compromise with society and quite simple to say nothing. But to take no stand *is* to take a stand—a stand for abortion, or at least for tolerating the status quo. Since the stance of neutrality contributes to the mentality that allows the practice, no one can be neutral on this issue.

D. Gareth Jones in *Brave New People* took a middle ground position on abortion. On some issues over which polarization has occurred, a third alternative—a middle ground position—is often to be preferred. But some issues do not allow for a third alternative. There was no middle ground on American slavery; there can be no middle ground on abortion. As the editor of *Christianity Today* has written:

> Maybe now Christians no longer need to puzzle about the absent witness of the church in Nazi Germany. Unless there is a Christian outcry against man's diminished dignity, history may once again repeat itself.[1]

We should understand by now that the distinctions of *process* and *potential* as used by proabortionists come from a world and life view foreign to Scripture. They are carefully selected words and concepts that on the surface seem enlightening but in the end serve to dehumanize the unborn. They are not scientific distinctions based on biological data; they are an interpretation of biological data from a naturalistic or humanistic perspective.

When evangelicals use these distinctions in the context of abortion, they are in fact borrowing their rationale from the prochoicers. Consequently, they serve to divide the evangelical community on this issue. In contrast, says Francis Schaeffer, "We must stand against the loss of humanness in all its forms."[2]

Scripture does not dissect individuals into "potential" and "actual" persons. It does not try to create two classes of human beings, one with value and the other with insufficient value for protection. The Bible does not suggest that we may kill those who may prove to be a burden to us. The kingdom of God knows no "quality of life" definitions of personhood.

Scripture places a transcendent value on all human life, not just "normal" life or life "wanted by society." Both victims of abortion—the tiny infant and the mother in distress—are of value to God. Indeed, every human life is viewed as precious in the sight of God because every person is created in the image of God. It does not matter how young or old, how small or big, how handicapped or perfectly formed, how poor or rich, how dark or light-skinned; the life of every individual is of value to God and should be of value to us.

This is the crux of the matter!

A CALL TO ACTION

It was Joseph Stalin who said, "One death is a tragedy; a million deaths is a statistic." Have abortions become a mere statistic for us?

The reality that abortion is indeed the violent killing of innocent human lives must be imprinted on our hearts and minds. It is not enough to agree that abortion is wrong. Sympathy for mother and child is not enough. Like Christ, we must enter the arena of suffering to effect change and healing. We must bear their burdens.

If we truly "love our neighbors"—women with problem pregnancies and the children in their wombs—we will sacrifice the comfort of our inaction. Rather than being worried about how the world perceives us (that is, "Are we open-minded and tolerant of the abortion point of view?"), we need to be concerned about what God thinks of us.

> Like a trampled spring and a polluted well
> Is a righteous man who gives way before the wicked
> (Proverbs 25:26).

On the other hand, Daniel 11:32 tells of a time when "the people who know their God will display strength and take action."

Defending and caring for the unborn and their parents will take strength and action, public action. For James asks,

> If a brother or sister is without clothing and in need
> of daily food, and one of you says to them, "Go in
> peace, be warmed and be filled," and yet you do not
> give them what is necessary for their body, what use
> is that? Even so faith, if it has no works, is dead,
> being by itself (2:15-17).

If righteous living requires that we give needy persons food and clothing, how much more should we seek to stop the killing of innocent human life? We might say the most eloquent things against abortion-on-demand; but such wonderful words, if without works, are dead. "Dear children, let us not love with words or tongue but with actions and in truth" (1 John 3:18, NIV).

In the Old Testament, God hid himself from Israel when they prayed and sacrificed yet failed to do justice:

> "What are your multiplied sacrifices to Me?"
> Says the LORD.
> "I have had enough of burnt offerings of rams,
> And the fat of fed cattle.
> And I take no pleasure in the blood of bulls, lambs,
>   or goats.
> When you come to appear before Me,
> Who requires of you this trampling of My courts?
> Bring your worthless offerings no longer,
> Incense is an abomination to Me.
> New moon and sabbath, the calling of assemblies—
> I cannot endure iniquity and the solemn assembly.
> I hate your new moon festivals and your appointed
>   feasts,
> They have become a burden to Me.
> I am weary of bearing them.
> So when you spread out your hands in prayer,
> I will hide My eyes from you,
> Yes, even though you multiply prayers,
> I will not listen.
> Your hands are covered with blood"
>   (Isaiah 1:11-15).

Iniquity in their instance was that they did not seek justice, reprove the ruthless, defend the fatherless, plead for the widow— basic acts of justice. Does God now tolerate a lack of concern for justice on our part?

We might be tempted to isolate ourselves from the abortion problem. After all, look at all the evils in the world— pornography, racial hatred, abuse of the poor, growing violence, immorality. We cannot isolate ourselves from any of these problems. We must address them. Yet what ought to be at the top of that list of evils is the daily destruction of so many little children. As we are instructed in Proverbs 31:8 (NIV):

> "Speak up for those who cannot speak for themselves,
> for the rights of all who are destitute."

This was the verse Dietrich Bonhoeffer used when he challenged the German evangelical church to come to the defense of the Jews. As we now know, the church in Germany did not respond. There were many reasons for their inaction—a total separation of church and state in their theology, anti-Semitism in their hearts, and the fear of being persecuted if they were to speak out. As a result, the German evangelical church emerged from World War II clothed in shame.

We face a similar challenge today. As Curt Young of the Christian Action Council has pleaded:

> Some Christians no doubt will see the question of abortion as a peripheral matter to the "business of the church." They will not recognize that the integrity of the church and its witness for generations is at stake.[3]

There can be no doubt that those presently trying to stop abortion are in fact those now pursuing justice for the weak and defenseless. Likewise, they are working to develop Crisis Pregnancy Centers and similar agencies to help women in need. The present prolife movement is putting their money, time, and effort where it is needed.

They do not deserve the criticism handed down by some evangelicals that they are not doing enough for women with problem pregnancies. These volunteers are doing their utmost. Indeed, the armchair critics who make such charges need to examine their own lives. Are they doing anything to stop abortions or to reach out to these women?

Consider this analogy. After the Beirut massacre at the Sabra and Shatilla camps by the Phalangists in 1982, the West was struck by the Kahan Commission's report. The purpose of the Commission had been to investigate the massacre to see if the Jewish commanders and forces had done anything wrong.

The Commission concluded that while the Jewish forces were not directly involved in the massacre, they were still guilty of "indirect responsibility." The idea is familiar: by doing nothing to prevent a wrong act, in spite of being in a position to do so, one shares a portion of the blame. Thomas Aquinas called it the "sin of omission." Modern domestic law refers to it as "negligence."[4]

Jews are especially aware, and painfully so, of the principle of indirect responsibility and how it works. They have so often watched the world stand by in silence while they were being discriminated against and openly slaughtered. When Defense Minister Ariel Sharon heard the verdict, he called it "the mark of Cain" on his life. (It was Cain who said, "Am I my brother's keeper?") The Talmud states unequivocally: "He who has the power to protest against a wrong . . . and does not do so . . . is guilty of the wrong committed" (Shabbat 546).

The prophet Ezekiel was even more explicit:

> " 'But if the watchman sees the sword coming and does not blow the trumpet to warn the people and the sword comes and takes the life of one of them, that man will be taken away because of his sin, but I will hold the watchman accountable for his blood' " (33:6, NIV)

To be indifferent to the death of unborn children is to be guilty of indirect responsibility—to have the "mark of Cain" on our life—and we will be held accountable for their blood. For we all know what is taking place. We cannot excuse ourselves by saying, "I didn't know . . . I had no idea what was going on."

These are times that call for extraordinary action by the church of Jesus Christ. God is giving us the strength and wisdom to respond with a united voice against abortion—and he will render to every man according to his works.

Conclusion, Notes

1. "Beyond Personal Piety," *Christianity Today*, 16 November 1979), 13. Actually, history is repeating itself in holocaust proportions with the death already of over eighteen million unborn children, together with a growing number of infants and elderly people.

2. Francis A. Schaeffer and C. Everett Koop, *Whatever Happened to the Human Race?* (Old Tappan, N.J.: Fleming H. Revell Co., 1979), 198.

3. Curt Young, *The Least of These* (Chicago: Moody Press, 1983), 201.

4. Hertzel Fishman, "Kahan Inspired by Judaism," and Allan E. Shapiro, "Sharon's Mark of Cain," both in *The Jerusalem Post*, 2 March 1983, 8; Roger Rosenblatt, "The Commission Report: The Law of the Mind," *Time*, 21 February 1983, 17.

Scripture Index

Subject Index

219